BIBLE PROVERBS FOR KIDS

Activity Book

Bible Proverbs for Kids Activity Book

Bible Pathway Adventures® is a trademark of BPA Publishing Ltd.
Defenders of the Faith® is a trademark of BPA Publishing Ltd.

ISBN: 978-1-998142-00-2

Author: Pip Reid
Creative Director: Curtis Reid

For more Bible resources, including Activity Books and printables, visit our website at:

www.biblepathwayadventures.com

◇◆ INTRODUCTION ◆◇

Welcome to *Bible Proverbs for Kids Activity Book*! This exciting adventure through the Bible is designed to guide you on a journey through some of the most important lessons that God has to teach us. Packed with 15 engaging and thought-provoking lessons, each one centered around a Bible proverb and paired with a fascinating Bible story. These aren't just any stories, they're timeless tales of heroes, kings, and ordinary people, just like you and me, who lived extraordinary lives. From the perseverance of Nehemiah and the faith of David when he faced Goliath, to the generosity of the widow with her offering to the courage of Gideon - there's so much to learn and discover!

Bible Pathway Adventures helps educators teach children about the Biblical faith in a fun and engaging way. We do this via our Activity Books and printable activities – available for download on our website shop.biblepathwayadventures.com

Thanks for buying this Activity Book and supporting our ministry. Every book purchased helps us continue our work providing free discipleship resources to families and educators around the world.

The search for Truth is more fun than Tradition!

◇◇ TABLE OF CONTENTS ◇◇

HUMILITY

Proverbs 16:18 and the story of King Nebuchadnezzar

1. Lesson objectives:

Students will be able to summarize the key message of Proverbs 16:18, define humility and apply it to their daily lives, and understand how God humbled King Nebuchadnezzar.

2. Introduction:

Begin the lesson by introducing the concept of humility. Ask students to offer their definitions of humility. Explain that humility is like a secret superpower that helps us to admit when we're wrong, celebrate other people's efforts, and to be ready to learn new things.

◉ HUMILITY: A modest or low view of one's own importance; humbleness

Introduce Proverbs 16:18: "Pride goes before destruction, and a haughty spirit before a fall." Ask students to discuss this verse and how it relates to humility. Explain that today's lesson will focus on the Bible story of a king who was humbled by God.

3. Bible story:

Read and discuss the story of King Nebuchadnezzar from Daniel 4:28-37. King Nebuchadnezzar, a very proud king, is humbled by God when he becomes like a wild animal for seven years. Only when he repents and praises God does his reason return to him, and he becomes even greater than before.

4. Activities:

* Bible story: King Nebuchadnezzar
* Bible quiz: Nebuchadnezzar restored
* Bible word search puzzle: Nebuchadnezzar praises God
* Worksheet: What's the Word?
* Bible verse coloring page: Proverbs 16:18
* Worksheet: Practising humility
* Creative writing: From pride to humility

King Nebuchadnezzar

King Nebuchadnezzar was up on the roof of his big palace in Babylon. He looked around, feeling very proud, and thought out loud, "Look at this city of Babylon that I've built all by myself with my own strong hands. Isn't it an awesome royal home, showing off how great I am?" Just as he finished talking, a voice seemed to drop down from heaven. "King Nebuchadnezzar! Here's some news for you: You're not going to be the king anymore. You're going to have to live out in the wild, away from other people, like an animal. You'll be eating grass, just like an ox, and this will last for seven different times, until you realize who really controls the kingdoms of men and chooses who gets to be in charge."

Without wasting a moment, these words came true. King Nebuchadnezzar left the people and started living like an animal, even eating grass! His body was often wet from the dew at night, and his hair grew so long it looked like eagle feathers. His nails turned as long and sharp as bird claws.

At the end of the days, Nebuchadnezzar looked up to the sky and his understanding returned. He thanked and praised God who lives forever. He understood that God's rule is forever, and that compared to God, everyone on Earth was unimportant. God does what He wants in heaven and on Earth, and no one can stop Him or question Him about what He's doing.

At this point, Nebuchadnezzar's officials came to find him, and he was back in charge of his kingdom, even more grand than before. So, Nebuchadnezzar, now a wiser and humbler king, praised and honored the King of Heaven. He understood that everything God does is right, His ways are fair, and if anyone acts too proud, God has the power to humble them.

Nebuchadnezzar RESTORED

Read Daniel 4:28-37. Answer the questions below.

1. Where was King Nebuchadnezzar when he spoke about the greatness of Babylon?

2. What did the king claim to have done in Babylon?

3. What message did a voice from heaven give to King Nebuchadnezzar?

4. How long was Nebuchadnezzar destined to live with the beasts of the field?

5. What physical changes occurred to King Nebuchadnezzar while he lived among the beasts?

6. What happened to the king at the end of the days?

7. Who is the King of heaven according to Nebuchadnezzar?

8. What returned to Nebuchadnezzar along with his reason?

9. Who sought Nebuchadnezzar after his reason returned to him?

10. What lesson did the king learn from his experience?

Nebuchadnezzar PRAISES GOD

Read Daniel 4:28-37. Find and circle the words below.

```
G B E A S T S R P M J U Z E C
S D P A N D P O R K H N H P O
M Q O T G I X O I P S T U H U
N A E M M L F J D Z I P M E N
G A J T I W E B E K T K B A S
A T O E I N O S P V D B L V E
X M N M S Z I N S R F P E E L
R B A O W T R O K O V B C N O
J A O D S A Y A N P Q G Y S R
C B H I K I N G D O M F U H S
W Y L J F H O Z O S R I D U B
S L N Z S H C S T I L N I U F
V O W W E Q R B G R A S S N O
X N Q X N K B U O D Z P S G X
N E B U C H A D N E Z Z A R L
```

KINGDOM

HUMBLE

EAGLES

BEASTS

NEBUCHADNEZZAR

COUNSELORS

MAJESTY

BABYLON

HEAVEN

DOMINION

GRASS

PRIDE

What's the Word?

Read Daniel 4:27-33 (ESV). Using the words below,
fill in the blanks to complete the Bible passage.

NEBUCHADNEZZAR	ROYAL	BODY	HEAVEN	PALACE
KINGDOM	DWELLING	BEASTS	GRASS	BABYLON

" All this came upon King .... At the end of twelve months he was walking on the roof of the royal .... of Babylon, and the king answered and said, "Is not this great ...., which I have built by my mighty power as a .... residence and for the glory of my majesty?" While the words were still in the king's mouth, there fell a voice from heaven, "O King Nebuchadnezzar, to you it is spoken: The .... has departed from you, and you shall be driven from among men, and your .... shall be with the .... of the field. And you shall be made to eat grass like an ox, and seven periods of time shall pass over you, until you know that the Most High rules the kingdom of men and gives it to whom he will." Immediately the word was fulfilled against Nebuchadnezzar. He was driven from among men and ate .... like an ox, and his .... was wet with the dew of .... till his hair grew as long as eagles' feathers, and his nails were like birds' claws. "

"Pride goes before destruction, and a haughty spirit before a fall."

(Proverbs 16:18)

Understanding humility

Read Proverbs 16:18 and answer the questions below.

What do you think Proverbs 16:18 means?

....

Can you remember a time when you were too proud? What happened?

....

How does Proverbs 16:18 and the story of King Nebuchadnezzar warn about the dangers of pride and encourage humility?

....

....

Give two examples where you can demonstrate humbleness in your daily life.

....

....

Practicing humility:

Find a jar (or a small box) and some decorative materials. Decorate your jar and label it 'Humility Jar'. Over the week, write down moments when you demonstrated humility on small pieces of paper, and put them in your jar. At the end of the week, share your experiences with your classmates or family.

From pride to humility

Read the story of King Nebuchadnezzar (Daniel 4:28-37).
Using the vocabulary below, rewrite this story in your own words.

....
....
....
....
....
....
....
....
....
....
....
....

PALACE   VOICE

MAJESTY   HUMBLE

KINGDOM   HONOR

FAITH

Proverbs 18:10 and the story of David and Goliath

1. Lesson objectives:

Students will be able to summarize the key message of Proverbs 18:10, define faith, and retell the story of David & Goliath and understand how David's faith helped him battle a giant.

2. Introduction:

Begin the lesson by introducing the concept of faith. Ask students to offer their definitions of faith. Explain that having faith means trusting that God will protect us and help us, even when we're afraid or things are difficult.

⊙ FAITH: complete trust or confidence in someone or something

Introduce Proverbs 18:10: "The name of God is a strong tower; the righteous man runs into it and is safe." Ask students to discuss this verse and how it relates to faith. Explain that today's lesson will focus on the Bible story of David, a man who placed his faith in God and overcame a giant!

3. Bible story:

Read and discuss the story of David and Goliath from 1 Samuel 17. David had great faith in God. He trusted that God would help him, even when he faced a mighty giant like Goliath. His faith was so strong, he was able to defeat Goliath with a sling and a stone.

4. Activities:

* Bible story: Facing the giant
* Bible quiz: David & Goliath
* Bible word search puzzle: David & Goliath
* Worksheet: What's the Word?
* Bible verse coloring page: Proverbs 18:10
* Worksheet: Faith in action
* Creative writing: Facing the Giant

Facing the giant

The Philistines and Israelites were ready for battle. The Philistines' camp was in Socoh and the Israelites were camped in the Valley of Elah. The Philistines had a giant named Goliath, who wore heavy bronze armor. He called out to the Israelites, "Why have a full battle? Choose someone to fight me. If I win, you serve us. If he wins, we'll serve you." The Israelites' knees knocked with fear. They were greatly afraid!

But David, a shepherd from Bethlehem, was full of faith and courage. When he arrived at the camp and heard about Goliath's challenge, he asked, "Who is this man defying God's army? What do we get if we beat him?" Saul, the leader of the Israelites, learned of David's courage and sent for him. David told Saul, "No one should be afraid. I'll fight Goliath." Saul did not believe David could defeat Goliath, but David explained how he'd fought off lions and bears to protect his sheep, and believed that God would help him against Goliath. So, David, with his staff, five stones, and a sling, went out to face Goliath.

Goliath made fun of David, but David was not scared. "You come against me with a sword and spear and javelin. But I come in God's name and He will deliver you into my hands." Goliath had heard enough. He raised his spear and stomped towards David. Clouds of dust rose with each step the giant made, but David wasn't afraid. He grabbed a stone from his bag, put it in his sling, and swung it above his head. *Whoosh! Whoosh! Whoosh!*

David aimed at the giant and let it fly. The stone whizzed through the air like a rocket and smacked Goliath in the middle of his huge, hairy forehead. Goliath stumbled forward and crashed to the ground. The Philistines stared in astonishment. They couldn't believe a young shepherd had just defeated their mighty giant, Goliath!

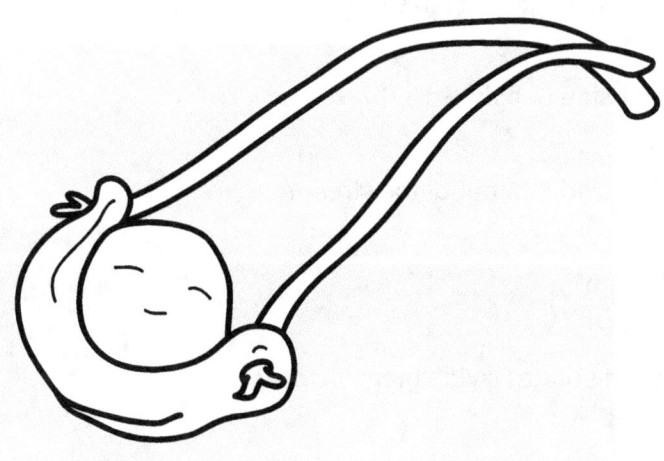

David & GOLIATH

Read 1 Samuel 15:1-18:7. Answer the questions below.

1. What was David's job when he was young?

2. Which prophet anointed David as king?

3. What musical instrument did David play for King Saul?

4. Where did the Israelite and Philistine armies set up camp?

5. How tall was Goliath?

6. How long did Goliath challenge Israel to send a man to fight him?

7. Who gave David permission to fight Goliath?

8. How many stones did David pick out of the stream?

9. How did David kill Goliath?

10. How did the Israelites celebrate David's great victory?

David & GOLIATH

Read 1 Samuel 15:1-18:7. Find and circle the words below.

```
G D K D I B J F M A O O N T R
O T J A H W E R H P C B Y A T
L J I V W V E J S H T D B F E
I K A I E R Z Q G I L I L I L
A G R D G G X F P L C S A V A
T A R G B Z T W O I K R X E H
H T D K A I X M Q S A A X S V
J O P P I R H X Y T R E I T A
V G P W Q N K S D I M L R O L
D T I S O O G G Z N O I N N L
O S Z A K U G S X E R T T E E
C Y Q Z N M B M A S P E Z S Y
O A Z L A T O Q Z U Q S Y Y Q
Z A R M Y L O W G C L G V M Q
S L I N G P S H E P H E R D Y
```

GIANT

DAVID

ELAH VALLEY

SLING

PHILISTINES

GOLIATH

ARMY

FIVE STONES

ISRAELITES

KING SAUL

SHEPHERD

ARMOR

What's the Word?

Read 1 Samuel 17:45-50 (ESV). Using the words below,
fill in the blanks to complete the Bible passage.

ISRAEL	PHILISTINE	SLING	BATTLE
DAVID	STONE	BEASTS	SAVES

" David said to Goliath, "You come to me with a sword and with a spear and with a javelin, but I come to you in the name of the Lord of hosts, the God of the armies of ...., whom you have defied. This day God will deliver you into my hand, and I will strike you down and cut off your head. I will give the dead bodies of the host of the Philistines this day to the birds of the air and to the wild .... of the earth, that all the earth may know that there is a God in Israel, and that all this assembly may know that God .... not with sword and spear. For the .... is God's, and He will give you into our hand." When the Philistine arose and came and drew near to meet David, David ran quickly toward the battle line to meet the Philistine. And .... put his hand in his bag and took out a stone and slung it and struck the Philistine on his forehead. The .... sank into his forehead, and he fell on his face to the ground. David prevailed over the Philistine with a .... and with a stone, and struck the .... and killed him. "

"The name of God is a strong tower; the righteous man runs into it and is safe."

(Proverbs 18:10)

Faith in action

Read Proverbs 18:10 and answer the questions below.

What do you think the 'strong tower' represents in this verse?

....

When David faced Goliath, how did he demonstrate his faith in God?

....

Can you think of a time when you demonstrated faith in God?
Write about it.

....

....

....

....

....

Faith in action:

Imagine you are David. What do you think you would
feel when facing Goliath? How would your faith help you?

....

....

....

....

....

Facing the giant

Read the story of David and Goliath (1 Samuel 17).
Using the vocabulary below, rewrite this story in your own words.

....

....

....

....

....

....

....

....

....

....

....

....

SLING	ARMIES OF ISRAEL
PHILISTINE	DAVID
DELIVER	VICTORY

GENEROSITY

Proverbs 11:25 and the story of the widow's offering

1. Lesson objectives:

Students will be able to explain the key message of Proverbs 11:25, define generosity, and retell the story of the widow's offering and what it reveals about the nature of true giving.

2. Introduction:

Begin the lesson by introducing the concept of generosity. Ask students to offer their definitions of generosity. Explain that generosity is more than giving gifts. It's about giving a part of yourself – time, effort, attention, or even a kind word.

◎ GENEROSITY: the quality of being kind and giving.

Introduce Proverbs 11:25: "A generous person will prosper; whoever refreshes others will be refreshed." Ask students to discuss this verse and how it relates to generosity. Explain that today's lesson will focus on the Bible story of a widow who gave everything she had.

3. Bible story:

Read and discuss the story of the widow's offering from Mark 12:41-44. A poor widow demonstrated generosity by giving all she had, two small coins, while many rich people gave large amounts but from their surplus.

4. Activities:

* Bible story: The widow's offering
* Bible quiz: The widow's offering
* Bible word search puzzle: The generous widow
* Worksheet: What's the Word?
* Bible verse coloring page: Proverbs 11:25
* Worksheet: A generous heart
* Creative writing: True riches in giving

The widow's offering

One day, while Yeshua was at the temple courts, a large crowd gathered to hear Him teach. He told them, "Watch out for the teachers who walk around in fancy clothes, love being greeted in public, and always sit in the best seats at gatherings. They take advantage of poor widows and pretend to be holy with their long prayers. These men will be punished most severely." Many in the crowd loved what Yeshua had to say, and listened to Him with delight.

After Yeshua had spoken, He sat near the donation box in the temple and watched as people dropped in their money. Many rich folks tossed in lots of coins. But then, a poor widow came and dropped in just two small copper coins, worth less than a penny. Yeshua gathered His disciples together and said, "Honestly, this poor widow has given more than all the rich people. They gave from their extras, but she, despite her poverty, gave everything she had, all that she had to live on." As Yeshua left the temple, one of His disciples said to Him, "Look, Teacher! What big stones! What magnificent buildings! Do you see all these great buildings?" He replied, "Not one stone here will be left on another; every single one will be thrown down."

The widow's OFFERING

Read Mark 12:35-44. Answer the questions below.

① Where was Yeshua teaching when he observed the crowd?

② What was Yeshua watching the crowd do?

③ Who gave large amounts of money?

④ Who put in two very small copper coins?

⑤ What did Yeshua say about the poor widow's offering?

⑥ According to Yeshua, what was different about the widow's offering compared to the others?

⑦ What can we learn from the widow's act of giving?

⑧ Provide an example of how you can be generous this week.

The generous WIDOW

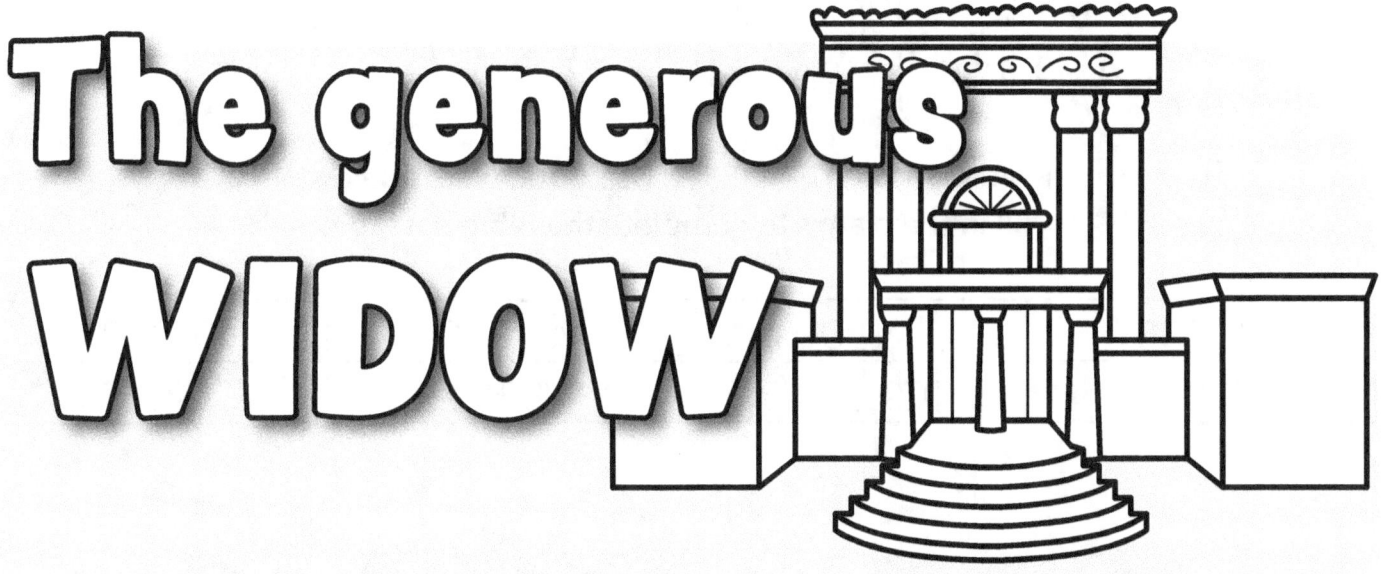

Read Mark 12:41-44. Find and circle the words below.

T	G	K	K	C	R	E	F	L	W	O	Z	P	J	P
K	E	E	U	Y	O	I	Y	M	Z	R	T	O	N	L
R	P	A	N	J	Q	P	C	Z	I	K	E	V	Q	U
K	A	C	C	E	F	K	P	H	B	J	M	E	O	C
D	H	Q	W	H	R	B	P	E	E	U	P	R	L	Q
J	I	N	F	Z	I	O	Q	G	R	B	L	T	J	Y
H	G	S	V	Z	F	N	S	N	M	Q	E	Y	A	E
Q	U	I	C	U	U	W	G	I	U	D	K	H	M	S
E	C	U	C	I	Z	D	I	L	T	D	Z	K	S	H
S	K	O	B	L	P	P	I	D	F	Y	J	V	W	U
X	A	W	I	Q	L	L	F	M	O	K	C	T	B	A
Q	E	I	I	N	Y	L	E	N	B	W	W	Y	I	C
T	N	X	E	K	S	U	L	S	T	M	K	J	O	C
X	D	O	Y	K	C	W	E	A	L	T	H	P	Y	Q
T	R	E	A	S	U	R	Y	E	M	H	S	R	N	S

COINS

DISCIPLES

RICH

TEACHING

TREASURY

TEMPLE

POVERTY

WEALTH

WIDOW

GENEROSITY

YESHUA

COPPER

What's the Word?

Read Mark 12:41-44 (ESV). Using the words below,
fill in the blanks to complete the Bible passage.

TEMPLE	WIDOW	POVERTY	COPPER
MONEY	DISCIPLES	YESHUA	CROWD

" While .... was teaching in the .... courts, he sat down opposite the place where the offerings were put and watched the .... putting their .... into the temple treasury. Many rich people threw in large amounts. But a poor .... came and put in two very small .... coins, worth only a few cents. Calling his .... to him, Yeshua said, "Truly I tell you, this poor widow has put more into the treasury than all the others. They all gave out of their wealth; but she, out of her ...., put in everything—all she had to live on." "

"A generous person will prosper; whoever refreshes others will be refreshed."

(Proverbs 11:25)

The generous heart

Read Proverbs 11:25 and 2 Corinthians 9:7. Answer the questions below.

Proverbs 11:25 says, "A generous person will prosper; whoever refreshes others will be refreshed." What do you think this means? Write down your thoughts:

....

....

2 Corinthians 9:7 states, "Each of you should give what you have decided in your heart to give, not reluctantly or under compulsion, for God loves a cheerful giver." How can you apply this verse in your daily life? Write down two examples:

....

....

Draw a picture of a time you were generous to someone else. Describe what happened and how it made you feel.

Generosity brainstorm:

Think about how you can be generous to someone this week.
Write down your idea here:

....

True riches in giving

Read the story of the widow's offering (Mark 12:41-44).
Using the vocabulary below, rewrite this story in your own words.

....

....

....

....

....

....

....

....

....

....

....

....

....

WIDOW	RICH
OFFERING	POOR
COINS	TREASURY

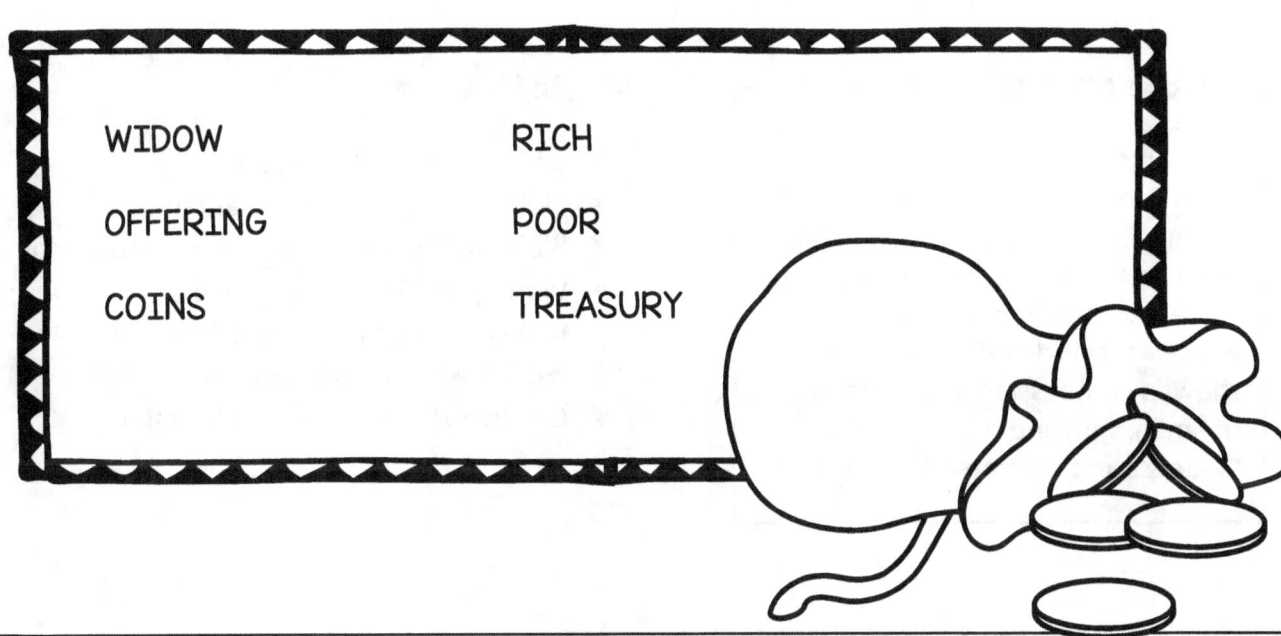

KINDNESS

Proverbs 21:21 and the story of the good Samaritan

1. Lesson objectives:

Students will be able to explain the key message of Proverbs 21:21, define kindness, and relate this understanding to the Good Samaritan's actions.

2. Introduction:

Begin the lesson by introducing the concept of kindness. Ask students to offer their definitions of kindness. Explain that kindness is showing care, compassion, and consideration for others.

◎ KINDNESS: the quality of being friendly, generous, and considerate

Introduce Proverbs 21:21: "Whoever pursues righteousness and kindness will find life, righteousness, and honor." Ask students to discuss this verse and how it relates to kindness. Explain that today's lesson will focus on the Bible story of a Samaritan who showed kindness to a stranger.

3. Bible story:

Read and discuss the story of the good Samaritan from Luke 10:25-37. A man who was beaten and left half-dead on the road. While religious leaders passed him by, a Samaritan, who was considered an outsider, showed compassion and cared for the man, showing the importance of kindness and helping others in need.

4. Activities:

* Bible story: The good Samaritan
* Bible quiz: The good Samaritan
* Bible word search puzzle: The good Samaritan
* Worksheet: What's the Word?
* Bible verse coloring page: Proverbs 21:21
* Worksheet: Kindness counts!
* Creative writing: Kindness in action

The good Samaritan

A Torah teacher decided to test Yeshua and asked, "Teacher, what should I do to live forever?" Yeshua replied, "What does the law say? How do you understand it?" The man answered, "You should love God with all your heart, soul, strength, and mind. Also, love your neighbor just like you love yourself." Yeshua said, "You're right! If you do this, you will truly live."

Wanting to make himself look good, the man asked another question. "Who exactly is my neighbor?" Yeshua replied, "A man was traveling from Jerusalem to Jericho when he was attacked by thieves. They stole his belongings, beat him up, and left him almost dead. A priest was also on that road, saw the man, but passed by without helping. A Levite did the same thing. But then, a Samaritan saw the man. He felt sorry for him, treated his injuries with oil and wine, put him on his own animal, and took him to an inn to take care of him.

The next day, the Samaritan gave the innkeeper some money and said, 'Take care of him. If you spend more, I'll pay you back when I return.' So, which of these three, do you think, was a real neighbor to the injured man?" The man replied, "The one who showed kindness." Yeshua said, "Go and do the same."

The good SAMARITAN

Read Luke 10:25-37. Answer the questions below.

1. Who asked Yeshua how to inherit eternal life?

2. How did Yeshua answer this man in Luke 10:27?

3. In this parable, where was the traveler going?

4. What happened to the traveler on this road?

5. Who was the first man to walk past?

6. Who was the second man to walk past?

7. Who was the third man to see the traveler?

8. What did the Samaritan do to help the traveler?

9. How much did he pay the innkeeper?

10. In this parable, who was the neighbor?

The good SAMARITAN

Read Luke 10:25-37 (ESV). Find and circle the words below.

```
Z G F U V M Q M L Y P Q O M J
S A M A R I T A N S E M P W E
T O R A H T E A C H E R I F R
Q K R H H J O A D F K U L P I
J Q Q V M B I O G F W N R L C
V E Y Y J L J X E Y P L O E H
J A S C Q W J R A S R K A V O
U X N U B Y B Y L M I L D I Q
O P R I N X C D W E E U Z T O
Z D S M M V N T O R S D U E J
P M J H M A K X U C T G R R P
M V E B Z H L T N Y U P V X N
Z V Z I N N S K D C E S P H R
H R O B B E R S S U L W F V D
D E N A R I I V X P Y F R P P
```

ROAD

JERICHO

ROBBERS

SAMARITAN

WOUNDS

PRIEST

ANIMAL

INN

MERCY

LEVITE

TORAH TEACHER

DENARII

What's the Word?

Read Luke 10:25-37 (ESV). Using the words below,
fill in the blanks to complete the Bible passage.

NEIGHBOR	LEVITE	DENARII	ANIMAL
JERUSALEM	COMPASSION	MERCY	ROBBERS

> The Torah teacher, desiring to justify himself said to Yeshua, "Who is my...............................?" Yeshua replied, "A man was going down from .... to Jericho and fell among robbers, who stripped him, beat him and departed, leaving him half dead. Now by chance a priest was going down that road, and when he saw him he passed by on the other side. Likewise, a .... when he came to the place and saw him, passed by on the other side. But a Samaritan, as he journeyed, came to where he was and when he saw him, he had .... He bound up his wounds, pouring on oil and wine. Then he set him on his own .... and brought him to an inn and took care of him. The next day he took out two .... and gave them to the innkeeper, saying, 'Take care of him, and whatever more you spend I will repay you when I come back.' Which of these three do you think proved to be a neighbor to the man who fell among the .... ?" He said, "The one who showed him ...." And Yeshua said to him, "Go and do likewise."

"Whoever pursues righteousness and kindness will find life, righteousness, and honor."

(Proverbs 21:21)

Kindness counts!

Read Proverbs 21:21 and answer the questions below.

Read Proverbs 21:21:

"Whoever pursues righteousness and kindness will find life, righteousness, and honor." What do you think this verse means?

....

Showing kindness:

In the parable of the good Samaritan, explain how the Samaritan showed kindness to a stranger.

....

....

....

....

....

Kindness challenge:

Write down three new acts of kindness you would like to try in the next week. Share your challenge with a friend or family member and encourage them to join you.

....

....

....

Kindness in action

Read the parable of the good Samaritan (Luke 10:25-37).
Using the vocabulary below, rewrite this parable in your own words.

....
....
....
....
....
....
....
....
....
....
....

SAMARITAN	JERICHO
TRAVELER	INNKEEPER
LEVITE	NEIGHBOR

HONESTY

Proverbs 12:22 and the story of Ananias and Sapphira

1. Lesson objectives:

Students will be able to explain the key message of Proverbs 12:22, define honesty, and retell the events of Ananias and Sapphira's dishonesty and the consequences they faced.

2. Introduction:

Begin the lesson by introducing the concept of honesty. Ask students to offer their definitions of honesty. Explain that honesty means telling the truth, even when it might be easier or less scary to tell a little lie.

◎ HONESTY: the quality of being truthful and sincere

Introduce Proverbs 12:22: "Lying lips are an abomination to God, but those who act faithfully are His delight." Ask students to discuss this verse and how it relates to honesty. Explain that today's lesson will focus on the Bible story of Ananias and Sapphira, a married couple who were dishonest, and the consequences that followed their actions.

3. Bible story:

Read and discuss the story of Ananias and Sapphira from Acts 4:32-5:11. In the early church community, believers shared all possessions, selling their property and giving the money to the apostles for distribution to those in need. Ananias and Sapphira sold their property but secretly kept back part of the money, while claiming to have given everything. When their lie was revealed, they each fell dead.

4. Activities:

* Bible story: Ananias & Sapphira
* Bible quiz: Ananias & Sapphira
* Bible word search puzzle: Divine judgment
* Worksheet: What's the Word?
* Bible verse coloring page: Proverbs 12:22
* Worksheet: A lesson in honesty
* Creative writing: Walking in truth

Ananias and Sapphira

In Jerusalem, the community of believers were really close, like one big family. They shared everything they had - no one said, "This is mine." Because those who had extra land or houses sold them and gave the money to the apostles, no one was poor. For example, Joseph, who was also known as Barnabas, sold his field and handed them the money. The apostles then helped whoever was in need.

However, a man named Ananias and his wife Sapphira sold some property they owned. Instead of giving the apostles all of the proceeds, they kept some back for themselves and only gave them some of the money. Peter, one of the apostles, said to Ananias, "Why did you lie to the Holy Spirit and keep some of the money? You haven't lied to us, but to God." When Ananias heard this, he fell down dead. This scared everyone who heard about it. Some young men came, wrapped him up, and buried him.

About three hours later, his wife came in, not knowing what happened. Peter asked her, "Did you sell the land for this much money?" She said, "Yes, that's right." But Peter said to her, "Why did you both decide to test the Spirit? The same men who buried your husband will carry you out, too." Just then, she fell down dead at his feet. The young men came in, found her there, and buried her next to her husband. And a great fear came upon the whole church and everyone who heard this story.

Ananias &
SAPPHIRA

Read Acts 4:32-5:11. Answer the questions below.

1. How is the unity of the early believers described in the Bible?

2. What does the Bible say about the finances of the believers?

3. How was the money from the sold lands and houses used?

4. Who is Joseph, also called Barnabas, and what did he do?

5. Who were Ananias and Sapphira and what did they do?

6. What happened to Ananias after Peter confronted him?

7. How long after Ananias's death did Sapphira enter?

8. How did Sapphira respond to Peter's question about the price of the land?

9. What was Sapphira's fate?

10. What effect did the deaths of Ananias and Sapphira have on the community and those who heard about it?

www.biblepathwayadventures.com
Bible Proverbs for Kids Activity Book

© BPA Publishing Ltd 2023

Divine JUDGMENT

Read Acts 4:32-5:11. Find and circle the words below.

```
F E X H V A S O X C H B D F N
T P A E P N V F F H O A V B E
K E D P H A P D W S L N J C E
E Z S W O E G E O U Y A S T D
P O B T J S P P Q B S N J Y Y
W E G A I Y T L H Q P I R R T
V K T W R M E L F H I A A Z E
C Y J E V N O X E L R S O B Z
R M B D R C A N E S I C D U A
R O I C J T W B Y Y T Y E Y O
P R O P E R T Y A W Q E A Z Z
R G U O A G C M S S V E T Z V
C E H S A P P H I R A M H O F
C R X H Q Y N F N F I E L D W
V T E D I S T R I B U T E J Z
```

APOSTLES

DEATH

PETER

FIELD

HOLY SPIRIT

PROPERTY

DISTRIBUTE

TESTIMONY

BARNABAS

NEEDY

ANANIAS

SAPPHIRA

What's the Word?

Read Acts 5:1-11 (ESV). Using the words below,
fill in the blanks to complete the Bible passage.

ANANIAS	SPIRIT	HEART	PETER	HUSBAND
DEED	SAPPHIRA	FEAR	CHURCH	PROCEEDS

" A man named .... and his wife .... sold a piece of property, and with his wife's knowledge he kept back for himself some of the proceeds and brought only a part of it and laid it at the apostles' feet. Peter said, "Ananias, why has Satan filled your .... to lie to the Holy Spirit and to keep back for yourself part of the .... of the land? While it remained unsold, did it not remain your own? And after it was sold, was it not at your disposal? Why is it that you have contrived this .... in your heart? You have not lied to man but to God." When Ananias heard these words, he fell down and breathed his last. And great .... came upon all who heard of it. The young men rose and wrapped him up and carried him out and buried him. After an interval of about three hours his wife came in, not knowing what had happened. Peter said to her, "Tell me whether you sold the land for so much." And she said, "Yes, for so much." But .... said to her, "How is it that you have agreed together to test the .... of God? Behold, the feet of those who have buried your .... are at the door, and they will carry you out." Immediately she fell down at his feet and breathed her last. When the young men came in they found her dead, and they carried her out and buried her beside her husband. And great fear came upon the whole .... and upon all who heard of these things. "

"Lying lips are an abomination to GOD, but those who act faithfully are His delight."

(Proverbs 12:22)

A lesson in honesty

Read Proverbs 12:22 and the story of Ananias and Sapphira in Acts 5:1-11.

Read Proverbs 12:22:

"Lying lips are an abomination to God, but those who act faithfully are His delight." What does this verse teach us about the importance of honesty?

....

Consequences of dishonesty:

Read Acts 5:1–11. Describe what Ananias and Sapphira did that was dishonest.

....

What were the consequences of their dishonesty?

....

Choosing honesty:

How does the message in Proverbs 12:22 relate to the story of Ananias and Sapphira from Acts 5:1–11?

....

Can you remember a time when you chose honesty, even when it was difficult? What happened?

....

Walking in truth

Read the story of Ananias and Sapphira (Acts 5:1-11).
Using the vocabulary below, rewrite this story in your own words.

....

....

....

....

....

....

....

....

....

....

....

ANANIAS	APOSTLES
HEART	PROPERTY
LIED	HOLY SPIRIT

PATIENCE

Proverbs 14:29 and the story of Abraham and Sarah

1. Lesson objectives:

Students will be able to explain the key message of Proverbs 14:29, define patience, and retell the story of Abraham and Sarah and what it reveals about patience and trusting God.

2. Introduction:

Begin the lesson by introducing the concept of patience. Ask students to offer their definitions of patience. Explain that patience is understanding that some things take time and can't be rushed, and it's being okay with waiting, even if waiting is hard.

◎ PATIENCE: the ability to wait or continue doing something despite difficulties

Introduce Proverbs 14:29: "Whoever is patient has great understanding, but one who is quick-tempered displays folly." Ask students to discuss this verse and how it relates to patience. Explain that today's lesson will focus on the Bible story of Abraham and Sarah, who demonstrated patience and received God's blessing.

3. Bible story:

Read and discuss the story of Abraham and Sarah from Genesis 18:1-15 and 21:1-7. Abraham and Sarah received a promise from God that they would have a child. Even though this seemed impossible because of their age, they stayed patient and kept their faith strong. After a long time waiting, they were blessed with a son named Isaac, showing that God's promise had come true.

4. Activities:

* Bible story: The miracle of patience
* Bible quiz: Sarah and Abraham
* Bible word search puzzle: Birth of Isaac
* Worksheet: What's the Word?
* Bible verse coloring page: Proverbs 14:29
* Worksheet: Understanding patience
* Creative writing: A promise kept

The miracle of patience

Abraham was sitting at the door of his tent near the oak trees of Mamre when he looked up and saw three men standing in front of him. He ran to them and bowed before them, saying, "Please, stay for a while. I will bring some water to wash your feet. You can rest under the trees. I will get some food for you, and you can eat as much as you want. Then you can continue your journey." The three men agreed to stay.

Abraham came to Sarah and said, "Quickly, prepare enough flour for three loaves of bread." He took his best young calf from his herd, had it cooked quickly, and served it to the men under the tree. While they were eating, the men asked Abraham about his wife. As Abraham pointed towards the tent, one of the men said, "I will return about the same time next year, and by then, Sarah will have a son."

Sarah, who was listening from inside the tent, couldn't believe her ears. She laughed to herself, thinking how it could be possible at their old age. But God heard her laugh and asked Abraham, "Why did Sarah laugh? Is anything too hard for Me? Just as I said, by this time next year, Sarah will have a son."

Later, God fulfilled His word to Sarah. Against all odds, Sarah became pregnant and gave birth to a son for Abraham, just as God had said she would. They named their son Isaac, which means 'he laughs'. Abraham was a hundred years old when Isaac was born, demonstrating that nothing is impossible for God.

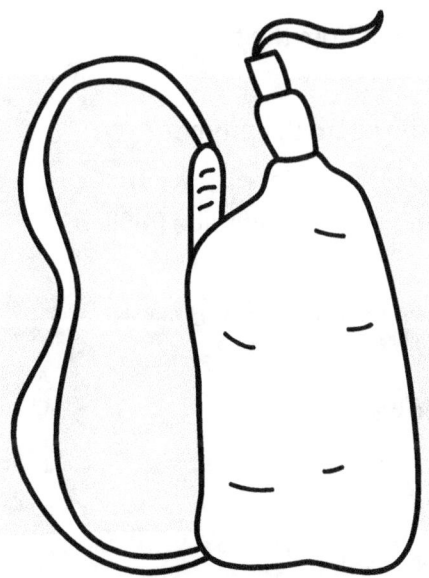

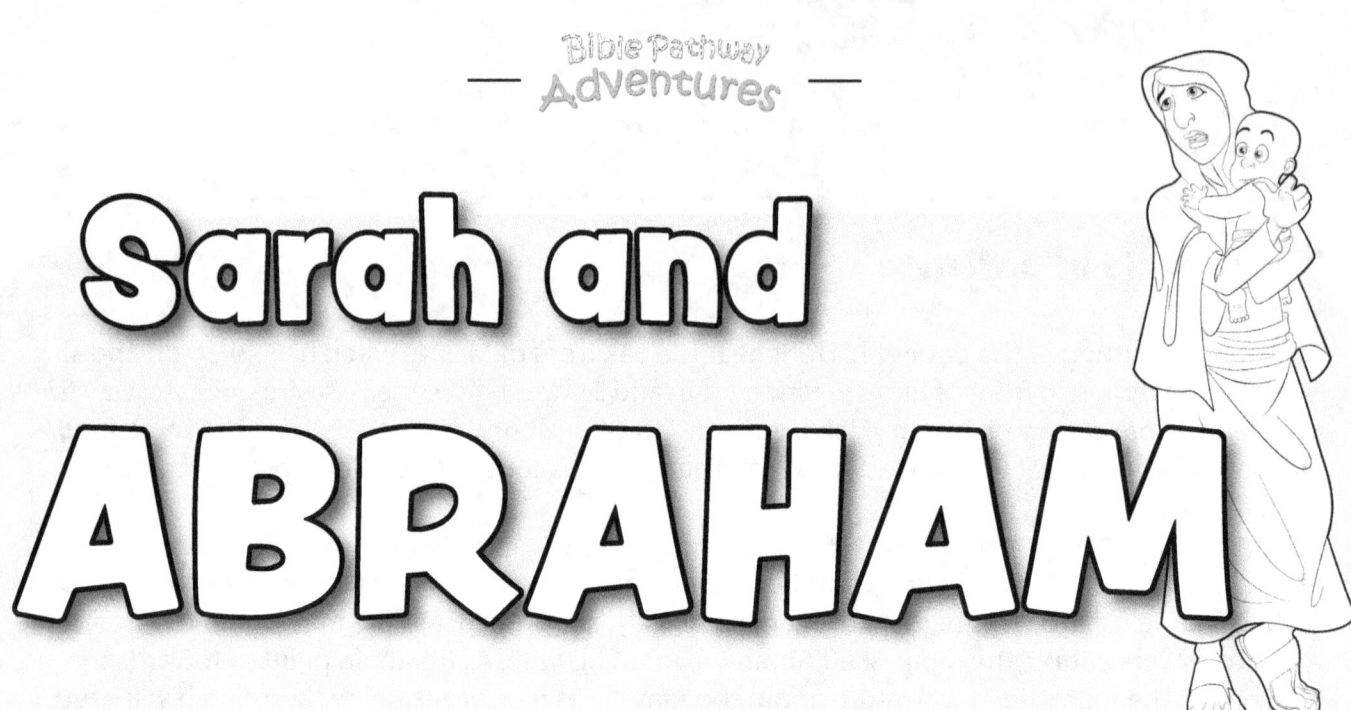

Sarah and ABRAHAM

Read Genesis 18:1-15 and 21:1-7. Answer the questions below.

1. Where was Abraham sitting when he saw the three men?

2. What did Abraham do when he saw the three men?

3. What did Abraham offer the three men?

4. Who were the three men who visited Abraham?

5. What promise was made to Abraham during this visit?

6. Who was listening to the conversation from the tent?

7. What was Sarah's reaction when she heard the promise?

8. What did God promise to Sarah and when was it to be fulfilled?

9. What was the name of the son born to Abraham and Sarah?

10. How old was Abraham when Isaac was born?

Birth of ISAAC

Read Genesis 18:1-15 and 21:1-7. Find and circle the words below.

M	I	L	O	P	Z	C	U	A	S	A	R	A	H	Y
H	I	Y	S	A	R	I	Y	R	N	W	J	I	A	Q
D	F	R	K	X	K	O	Y	T	H	S	L	S	U	N
S	C	M	A	X	D	S	M	M	I	F	D	A	U	X
X	O	P	P	C	H	N	O	I	I	Y	M	A	E	Q
I	Q	O	K	I	L	W	Z	F	S	U	L	C	B	O
J	O	Y	Z	D	M	E	K	U	M	E	L	K	T	I
K	W	Q	D	X	R	Y	U	L	U	A	A	T	F	E
N	A	B	R	A	H	A	M	G	A	M	M	W	I	I
J	J	H	Q	Q	Q	C	R	T	N	H	S	R	J	F
B	X	D	R	N	I	B	M	J	W	E	C	T	E	A
W	C	X	H	P	A	T	I	E	N	C	E	B	X	I
V	K	T	P	B	L	E	S	S	I	N	G	H	W	T
A	L	A	U	G	H	T	E	R	X	T	E	N	T	H
M	K	U	I	R	G	U	W	E	M	I	B	Y	N	O

PROMISE

OAKS OF MAMRE

PATIENCE

MIRACLE

ABRAHAM

BLESSING

LAUGHTER

SARAH

TENT

ISAAC

JOY

FAITH

What's the Word?

Read Genesis 18:1-14 (WEB). Using the words below,
fill in the blanks to complete the Bible passage.

OAKS	LAUGHED	BREAD	CALF	ABRAHAM
TENT	HERD	THREE	SARAH	SERVANT

" Yahweh appeared to him by the .... of Mamre, as he sat in the tent door in the heat of the day. He lifted up his eyes and looked, and saw that .... men stood near him. When he saw them, he ran to meet them from the tent door, and bowed himself to the earth, and said, "My lord, if now I have found favor in your sight, please don't go away from your servant. Now let a little water be fetched, wash your feet, and rest yourselves under the tree. I will get a piece of .... so you can refresh your heart. After that you may go your way, now that you have come to your servant." They said, "Very well, do as you have said." Abraham hurried into the tent to Sarah, and said, "Quickly prepare three seahs of fine meal, knead it, and make cakes." Abraham ran to the ...., and fetched a tender and good calf, and gave it to the .... He hurried to dress it. He took butter, milk, and the .... which he had dressed, and set it before them. He stood by them under the tree, and they ate. They asked him, "Where is Sarah, your wife?" He said, "There, in the tent." He said, "I will certainly return to you at about this time next year; and behold, Sarah your wife will have a son." Sarah heard in the .... door, which was behind him. Now .... and .... were old, well advanced in age. Sarah had passed the age of childbearing. Sarah .... within herself, saying, "After I have grown old will I have pleasure, my lord being old also?" Yahweh said to Abraham, "Why did Sarah laugh, saying, 'Will I really bear a child when I am old?' Is anything too hard for Yahweh? At the set time I will return to you, when the season comes around, and Sarah will have a son." "

"Whoever IS PATIENT has great understanding, but one who is QUICK-TEMPERED DISPLAYS FOLLY."

Proverbs 14:29

Understanding patience

Read Proverbs 14:29:

"Whoever is patient has great understanding, but one who is quick-tempered displays folly." What do you think this proverb means?

How can you apply the lesson of patience from the story of Abraham and Sarah in your own life?

....

A journey with Abraham and Sarah:

Think about the story of Abraham and Sarah. They had to be patient and wait many years for God's promise of a child to come true. How did Abraham and Sarah show patience or impatience?

....

Can you think of a time when you had to be patient? How did you feel?

....

What did you learn from having to wait?

....

Let's draw!

Draw a picture of a situation where you have to be patient. It could be a time when you're waiting for your turn, waiting for a special day, or any other situation where patience is required.

A promise kept

Read the story of Abraham and Sarah (Genesis 18:1-15 and 21:1-7).
Using the vocabulary below, rewrite this story in your own words.

....
....
....
....
....
....
....
....
....
....
....
....

SARAH	SERVANT
ABRAHAM	TENT
LAUGH	MEN

COURAGE

Proverbs 28:1 and the story of Gideon

1. Lesson objectives:

Students will be able to explain the key message of Proverbs 28:1, define courage, and understand how God views courage through the retelling of the Bible story, Gideon defeats Midian.

2. Introduction:

Begin the lesson by introducing the concept of courage. Ask students to offer their definitions of courage. Explain that courage isn't the absence of fear. It's about feeling afraid and choosing to do something anyway because you believe it's the right thing to do or because you want to overcome a challenge.

◎ COURAGE: the ability to control your fear in a dangerous or difficult situation

Introduce Proverbs 28:1: "The wicked flee though no one pursues, but the righteous are as bold as a lion." Ask students to discuss this verse and how it relates to courage. Explain that today's lesson will focus on the Bible story of Gideon, a man who demonstrated courage in the face of great danger.

3. Bible story:

Read and discuss the story of Gideon from Judges 6-7. Gideon, a man of little self-confidence, was called by God to lead an army against the Midianites. Despite his initial fear and doubt, Gideon mustered the courage to obey God's command, and with a small army of 300 men, he defeated the Midianites.

4. Activities:

* Bible story: Gideon defeats Midian
* Bible quiz: Gideon
* Bible word search puzzle: Gideon's army
* Worksheet: What's the Word?
* Bible verse coloring page: Proverbs 28:1
* Worksheet: Bold as a lion
* Creative writing: Courage and faith

Gideon defeats Midian

Early one morning, Gideon and the Israelites set up camp near the spring of Harod, with the enemy Midianites camping north of them. God spoke to Gideon, saying, "You've got too many men with you for this battle. If you win, you'll think it was all because of your own strength and not because I helped you. Tell everyone who's afraid to go home." Just like that, Gideon's army went from 32,000 to 10,000.

God said to Gideon, "Still too many. Let's see who's ready for battle. Take these men to the water and see how they drink." After this test, only 300 men were left. God promised, "With these 300, I will help you win the battle." Gideon sent the other men of Israel back to their homes, keeping only the 300. That night, God said to Gideon, "Don't worry, you've got this. If you're afraid, take your servant into the enemy camp and listen to what they are saying." So, Gideon and his servant went down to the edge of the camp. They arrived just as a man was telling a friend his dream. "I had a dream," he was saying. "A loaf of bread came rolling into the Midianite camp. It hit the tent so hard that the tent turned over and fell flat." His friend said, "This must be the sword of Gideon, the Israelite. God will let Gideon defeat the whole army of Midian."

Full of courage, Gideon went back to his camp and woke his men. "Get up! God has given us victory." He divided the 300 men into three groups, gave them trumpets (shofars), and jars with torches inside. He instructed them to follow his lead, "When I blow my shofar, you blow yours and shout, 'For God and for Gideon!'" In the middle of the night, the Israelites did exactly that. The Midianites woke up in panic and started fighting each other. Gideon's tiny army stood their ground, and the Midianites fled in terror. Gideon and the Israelites defeated the Midianites, just as God had promised.

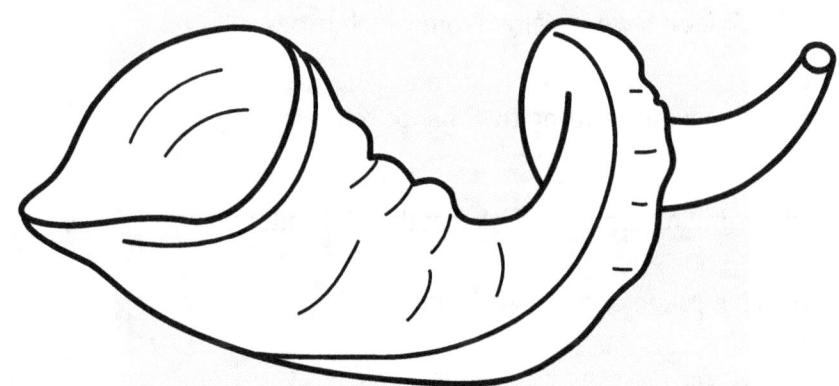

GIDEON

Read Judges 6:1-7:25. Answer the questions below.

1. Why did God allow the Midianites to attack the Israelites?

2. Where was Gideon threshing wheat?

3. What message did the Angel give Gideon?

4. What food did Gideon prepare as a sacrifice?

5. What Midianite altar did Gideon destroy?

6. What object did Gideon place on the ground to receive a sign from God?

7. How many soldiers did Gideon have initially? From which tribes of Israel?

8. How many men lapped the water, putting their hands to their mouths?

9. What objects did Gideon and his army use to defeat the Midianites?

10. What insect does the Bible use to describe the number of Midianites in their camp?

Gideon's ARMY

Read Judges 6:1-7:25. Find and circle each of the words below.

```
E J T L U H I Y M C O T M I G
V B Q O P U V X T A N D F S I
G G B U R F M Y T M O C B R D
A X Q K W C P I H P D W U A E
R K B R N C H D J O R A M E O
M G Y R I E R E C F I T V L N
E L V K T U E U S M N E L I W
D P Q T G S A L R I K R Y T I
M C F D L E U K S D J O S E F
E D N W M A K K L I W M E S B
N J S H O F A R H A T A F A V
P Y A H W E H U D N L X I S P
O H K Z S Y G U L L Y G M W V
I E B M O R E H H P K Q R K X
M K F O E M P T Y J A R S L V
```

ISRAELITES

GIDEON

YAHWEH

MOREH

KNEELS

CAMP OF MIDIAN

ARMED MEN

DRINK

TORCHES

WATER

EMPTY JARS

SHOFAR

What's the Word?

Read Judges 7:1-8 (ESV). Using the words below,
fill in the blanks to complete the Bible passage.

HAROD	DRINK	MIDIANITES	WATER	PEOPLE
GIDEON	MOUTHS	TRUMPETS	FEARFUL	LAPPED

“ Gideon and the people who were with him rose early and encamped beside the spring of .... The camp of Midian was north of them, by the hill of Moreh, in the valley. God said to ...., "The people with you are too many for me to give the .... into their hand, lest Israel boast over me, saying, 'My own hand has saved me.' Now therefore proclaim in the ears of the people, saying, 'Whoever is .... and trembling, let him return home and hurry away from Mount Gilead.'" Then 22,000 of the people returned, and 10,000 remained. God said to Gideon, "The people are still too many. Take them down to the ...., and I will test them for you there, and anyone of whom I say to you, 'This one shall go with you,' shall go with you, and anyone of whom I say to you, 'This one shall not go with you,' shall not go." So he brought the .... down to the water. God said to Gideon, "Every one who laps the water with his tongue, as a dog laps, you shall set by himself. Likewise, every one who kneels down to ...." The number of those who lapped, putting their hands to their ...., was 300 men, but the rest of the people knelt down to drink water. God said to Gideon, "With the 300 men who .... I will save you and give the Midianites into your hand, and let all the others go every man to his home." So the people took provisions in their hands, and their .... And he sent the rest of Israel every man to his tent, but retained the 300 men. ”

"The wicked flee though no one pursues, but the righteous are as bold as a lion."

(Proverbs 28:1)

Bold as a lion

Read Judges 6:36-7:25:

God chose Gideon to lead an army of 300 men against the Midianites. Using a unique strategy, He helped Gideon and his small army win the battle. Why do you think Gideon had courage?

....

....

Can you think of a time when you needed courage? Write about it.

....

....

Read Proverbs 28:1:

"The wicked flee when no one pursues, but the righteous are bold as a lion." What does it mean to be 'bold as a lion'?

....

....

Let's draw!

Draw a scene from the story of Gideon that shows his courage.

Courage is doing the right thing even when you are afraid. Have courage, just like Gideon!

Courage and faith

Read the story of Gideon (Judges 6:1-7:25).
Using the vocabulary below, rewrite this story in your own words.

....
....
....
....
....
....
....
....
....
....
....
....

GIDEON	WATER
TRUMPETS	ISRAEL
MIDIANITES	300

TRUST

Proverbs 3:5-6 and the story of Ruth and Naomi

1. Lesson objectives:

Students will be able to explain the key message of Proverbs 3:5-6, define trust, and understand the importance of trusting God through the story of Ruth.

2. Introduction:

Begin the lesson by introducing the concept of trust. Ask students to offer their definitions of trust. Explain that when someone shows they're reliable and honest over time, you learn to trust them. But if they break their promise or hurt you, trust can be damaged.

◉ TRUST: to believe that someone is good and honest, and will not harm you, or something is safe and reliable

Introduce Proverbs 3:5-6: "Trust God with all your heart, and do not lean on your own understanding. In all your ways acknowledge Him and He will make straight your paths." Ask students to discuss this verse and how it relates to trust. Explain that today's lesson will focus on the Bible story of Ruth, and how she demonstrated trust and loyalty.

3. Bible story:

Read and discuss the story of Ruth and Naomi in Ruth 1:1-22, a great example of trust and loyalty. During a time of famine, Naomi, who lost her husband and sons, decided to return to her hometown, Bethlehem. Her daughter-in-law Ruth chose to trust her and the God of Israel, and accompanied her back to Bethlehem, leaving her own land and people behind.

4. Activities:

* Bible story: A tale of loyalty and trust
* Bible quiz: Ruth & Naomi
* Bible word search puzzle: Ruth & Naomi
* Worksheet: What's the Word?
* Bible verse coloring page: Ruth 1:16
* Worksheet: Trust in action
* Creative writing: Trust in tough times

A tale of loyalty and trust

In a land called Moab, there was a special bond between two women named Ruth and Naomi. Naomi was an older woman, and she had faced a lot of sadness in her life, losing both her husband and her two sons. One of those sons had been married to Ruth. Instead of going back to her own family after her husband died, Ruth chose to stay with Naomi.

One day, Naomi heard that the famine in her hometown, Bethlehem, was over. She decided to return to her hometown. Ruth decided to go with her, even though it meant leaving her own land, people, and customs behind. She made a promise to Naomi, saying, "Where you go, I will go; where you stay, I will stay. Your people will be my people and your God will be my God." This showed an incredible amount of trust.

When the two women arrived in Bethlehem, Ruth worked hard to gather grain so they could eat. With Naomi's advice, Ruth eventually remarried a good man named Boaz and had a family of her own.

Ruth & NAOMI

Read Ruth 1:1-22. Answer the questions below.

1. Why did Elimelech and his family move to Moab?

2. What happened to Elimelech in Moab?

3. Who were the wives of Naomi's sons?

4. What made Naomi decide to return to Bethlehem?

5. How did Naomi's daughters-in-law initially react when she told them to go back to their families?

6. What was Naomi's reasoning behind telling Orpah and Ruth to return to Moab?

7. How did Ruth respond when Naomi told her to stay in Moab?

8. Who stayed in Moab and who traveled with Naomi to Bethlehem?

9. What was the reaction of the people of Bethlehem when Naomi and Ruth returned?

10. How did Ruth show her loyalty and trust to Naomi?

Ruth & NAOMI

Read Ruth 1:1-22. Find and circle each of the words below.

B	N	M	O	A	B	I	T	E	V	X	W	R	R	G
C	W	H	B	E	T	H	L	E	H	E	M	A	U	B
Q	G	U	V	F	L	H	K	X	T	E	W	T	T	W
F	B	D	Q	D	B	O	I	L	E	O	L	S	H	U
H	T	F	S	S	L	T	V	S	Q	V	O	W	F	L
O	F	P	L	W	I	N	Q	E	X	E	Y	F	E	K
A	G	E	U	M	I	B	T	P	J	M	A	V	P	C
M	O	T	H	E	R	I	N	L	A	W	L	W	C	V
W	F	F	X	K	M	A	Q	R	V	B	I	G	B	R
J	I	G	I	W	R	P	H	M	L	D	B	N	O	D
Q	E	D	H	O	P	U	F	Z	U	M	Y	U	A	U
F	S	H	O	Y	D	C	M	D	V	X	V	Z	Z	B
U	L	V	K	W	N	A	O	M	I	E	T	S	C	O
J	O	U	R	N	E	Y	G	F	A	M	I	N	E	M
L	B	A	R	L	E	Y	H	A	R	V	E	S	T	O

RUTH

NAOMI

WIDOW

FAMINE

BETHLEHEM

LOVE

JOURNEY

BOAZ

LOYAL

MOTHER-IN-LAW

MOABITE

BARLEY HARVEST

What's the Word?

Read Ruth 1:8-17 (ESV). Using the words below,
fill in the blanks to complete the Bible passage.

NAOMI	HUSBAND	RETURN	HUSBAND	VOICES
RUTH	ORPAH	LODGE	DAUGHTERS	BITTER

" Naomi said to her two daughters-in-law, "Go, return each of you to her mother's house. May God deal kindly with you, as you have dealt with the dead and with me. God grant that you may find rest, each of you in the house of her ....!" She kissed them, and they lifted up their voices and wept. They said to her, "No, we will return with you to your people." But .... said, "Turn back, my daughters; why will you go with me? Have I yet sons in my womb that they may become your husbands? Turn back, my ....; go your way, for I am too old to have a .... If I should say I have hope, even if I should have a husband this night and should bear sons, would you therefore wait till they were grown? Would you therefore refrain from marrying? No, my daughters, for it is exceedingly .... to me for your sake that the hand of God has gone out against me." They lifted up their .... and wept again. .... kissed her mother-in-law, but Ruth clung to her. And she said, "See, your sister-in-law has gone back to her people and to her gods; return after your sister-in-law." But .... said, "Do not urge me to leave you or to .... from following you. For where you go I will go, and where you .... I will lodge. Your people shall be my people, and your God my God. Where you die I will die, and there will I be buried. May God do so to me and more also if anything but death parts me from you." "

Where YOU GO, I WILL GO. Where you stay, I WILL STAY. Your people shall be my PEOPLE & YOUR GOD my GOD

(RUTH 1:16)

Ruth

Trust in action

Bible story:

In Moab, two women named Ruth and Naomi shared a unique bond. After Naomi lost her husband and sons, Ruth, her daughter-in-law, stayed by her side. When Naomi chose to return to Bethlehem, Ruth told her, "Where you go, I will go; where you stay, I will stay. Your people will be my people and your God my God." Later, in Bethlehem, Ruth worked hard, gathering grain to feed them both. With Naomi's guidance, she later married Boaz and began a new family.

1. Why was Ruth's decision to stay with Naomi an act of trust?

....

2. What did Ruth say to show her commitment to Naomi?

....

3. How did Ruth show her trust in Naomi once they arrived in Bethlehem?

....

"Trust God with all your heart, and do not lean on your own understanding. In all your ways acknowledge Him and He will make straight your paths." (Proverbs 3:5-6)

1. What do you think this proverb means?

....

2. How do you show God you trust Him?

....

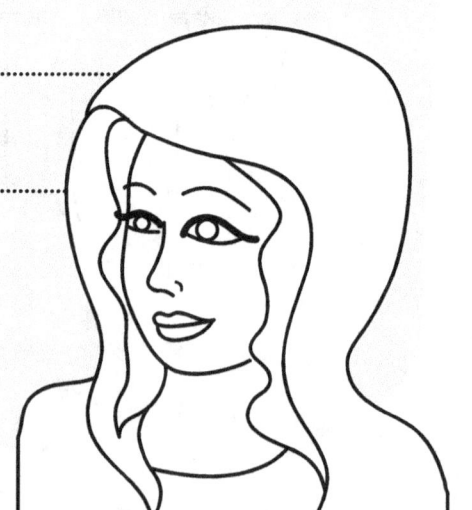

Trust in tough times

Read the story of Ruth and Naomi (Ruth 1:1-22)
Using the vocabulary below, rewrite this story in your own words.

....
....
....
....
....
....
....
....
....
....
....

RUTH	BETHLEHEM
NAOMI	GOD
DAUGHTER	MOTHER-IN-LAW

PERSEVERANCE

Proverbs 24:16 and the story of Nehemiah

1. Lesson objectives:

Students will be able to explain the key message of Proverbs 24:16, define perseverance, and retell the story of Nehemiah and what it reveals about having perseverance in tough times.

2. Introduction:

Begin the lesson by introducing the concept of perseverance. Ask students to offer their definitions of perseverance. Sometimes, things take time and a lot of effort. But if you have perseverance, you keep pushing forward, no matter the challenges. No matter how many times we face challenges or 'fall,' we can always get back up and try again.

⦿ PERSEVERANCE: to continue to do or achieve something, even when it is hard or takes a long time

Introduce Proverbs 24:16: "For the righteous falls seven times and rises again, but the wicked stumble in times of calamity." Ask students to discuss this verse and how it relates to perseverance. Explain that today's lesson and the Bible story of Nehemiah will focus on the importance of perseverance.

3. Bible story:

Read and discuss the story of Nehemiah in Nehemiah 1:1-6:19. Nehemiah, a man who served the king in a faraway land, heard the wall of Jerusalem had broken down and its gates were burnt. Feeling called by God, he bravely asked the king if he could go back to Jerusalem to help rebuild the wall. Despite facing many challenges, Nehemiah never gave up and led the people of Jerusalem to rebuild the wall, showing everyone the power of perseverance and faith.

4. Activities:

* Bible story: Nehemiah's challenge
* Bible quiz: Nehemiah
* Bible word search puzzle: Rebuilding of Jerusalem
* Worksheet: What's the Word?
* Bible verse coloring page: Proverbs 24:16
* Worksheet: The power of perseverance
* Creative writing: Faith and perseverance

Nehemiah's challenge

Long ago in the city of Jerusalem, the once mighty wall that protected its people lay in ruins. This was a big problem, as a city wall in those days was essential for safety. Enter Nehemiah, an ordinary guy with an important job in a faraway land. He was cupbearer to King Artaxerxes, the king of Persia. One day, he received the bad news. "Those who survived the exile and are back in the province are in great trouble and disgrace. The wall of Jerusalem is broken down, and its gates have been burned with fire." Heartbroken, Nehemiah decided to do something about it. After praying to God, he asked the king if he could return to Jerusalem and help rebuild the city. And the king said, "Yes!"

So, Nehemiah hurried home to Jerusalem. But the task was huge, and he faced many challenges. A group of people didn't want him to rebuild the wall and tried to stop him. But Nehemiah was persistent and inspired everyone around him to join in rebuilding their city. Brick by brick, day by day, they worked together.

Even when things got tough and enemies tried to stop him, Nehemiah stood firm, motivating everyone to keep pushing forward. Thanks to his perseverance, in just 52 days, the wall of Jerusalem was rebuilt. Remember, even when things get tough, keep going like Nehemiah!

NEHEMIAH

Read Nehemiah 1:1-4:23 and 6:1-8:18. Answer the questions below.

1. In what kingdom was Nehemiah living?

2. What was Nehemiah's job?

3. How did Nehemiah hear about news about Jerusalem?

4. What did Nehemiah ask the king of Persia?

5. What did Sanballat, Tobia and Gesham accuse Nehemiah of doing?

6. Who was the high priest?

7. Which men repaired the section of the wall over the Horse Gate?

8. How long did it take to rebuild the walls of Jerusalem?

9. What happened when the Israelites' enemies heard the walls were rebuilt?

10. In chapter 8, which Appointed Time (Feast) did the people celebrate?

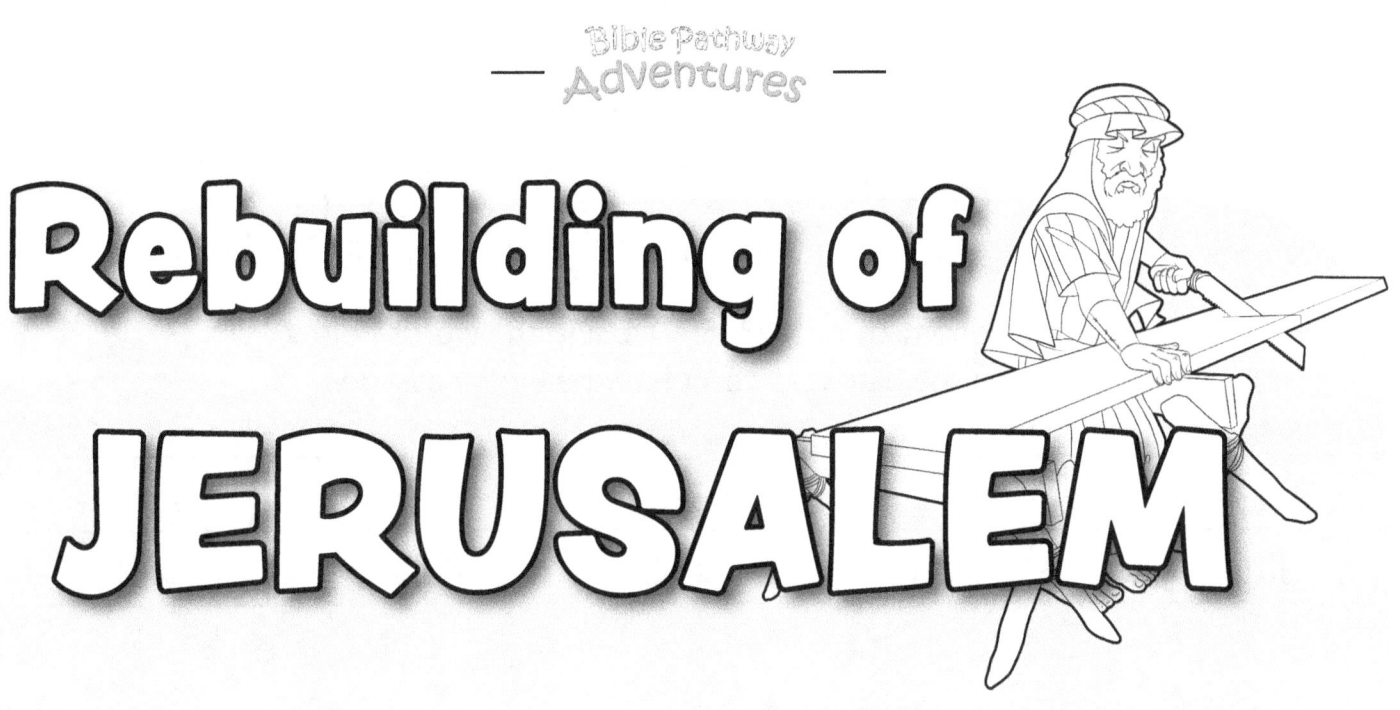

Rebuilding of JERUSALEM

Read Nehemiah 1:1-4:23. Find and circle the words below.

```
H I G H P R I E S T S M T B G
N N X D L E X Q S E A E A P J
E L I T R L A T M O N O L S E
H B Z C B E I U F I B H F H R
E F V G I N P A X M A W Y E U
M T F H P O G A C H L F V E S
I H F V L Q J U I D L S N P A
A U W E A P O N Q R A E Y G L
H L D D X Y D Z K W T M W A E
J J J R H G D S P C Y J A T M
T L A N D O F J U D A H L E O
T C V J B R F G U M N J L C Y
G A T E O F Y E S H A N A H S
G O D O F H E A V E N L E R G
K I N G A R T A X E R X E S G
```

NEHEMIAH

WEAPON

HIGH PRIEST

LAND OF JUDAH

WALL

SANBALLAT

JERUSALEM

REPAIR

GOD OF HEAVEN

KING ARTAXERXES

GATE OF YESHANAH

SHEEP GATE

What's the Word?

Read Nehemiah 4:15-23 (ESV). Using the words below,
fill in the blanks to complete the Bible passage.

ENEMIES	DAWN	SPEARS	BURDENS	BUILDERS
JUDAH	SERVANTS	SWORD	JERUSALEM	WORK

" When our .... heard that it was known to us and that God had frustrated their plan, we all returned to the wall, each to his work. From that day on, half of my servants worked on construction, and half held the spears, shields, bows, and coats of mail. And the leaders stood behind the whole house of ...., who were building on the wall. Those who carried .... were loaded in such a way that each labored on the work with one hand and held his weapon with the other. And each of the .... had his .... strapped at his side while he built. The man who sounded the trumpet was beside me. I said to the nobles and to the officials and to the rest of the people, "The .... is great and widely spread, and we are separated on the wall, far from one another. In the place where you hear the sound of the trumpet, rally to us there. Our God will fight for us." So, we labored at the work, and half of them held the .... from the break of .... until the stars came out. I also said to the people at that time, "Let every man and his servant pass the night within ...., that they may be a guard for us by night and may labor by day." So, neither I nor my brothers nor my .... nor the men of the guard who followed me, none of us took off our clothes… "

"For the righteous falls seven times and rises again, but the wicked stumble in times of calamity."

(Proverbs 24:16)

The power of perseverance

Read Proverbs 24:16:

"For the righteous falls seven times and rises again, but the wicked stumble in times of calamity." How do you think this proverb relates to Nehemiah's story?

....

Write about a time when you persevered, even though it was difficult.

....

....

Draw a four-panel comic strip of Nehemiah's story. Here are some ideas for the panels:

* Nehemiah receiving the news about Jerusalem.

* Nehemiah asking the King for his permission and help.

* Nehemiah rallying the people of Jerusalem to help him rebuild.

* The completion of Jerusalem's wall despite all the opposition.

Perseverance is about never giving up, even when things get tough. Write a short paragraph about how you can show more perseverance in your own life.

....

....

Faith and perseverance

Read the story of Nehemiah (Nehemiah 1:1-8:19).
Using the vocabulary below, rewrite this story in your own words.

....
....
....
....
....
....
....
....
....
....
....
....
....

NEHEMIAH	GATE OF YESHANA
JERUSALEM	SANBALLAT
HIGH PRIEST	KING

INTEGRITY

Proverbs 10:9 and the story of Job

1. Lesson objectives:

Students will be able to explain the key message of Proverbs 10:9, define integrity, and retell the story of Job and how his integrity pleased God.

2. Introduction:

Begin the lesson by introducing the concept of integrity. Ask students to offer their definitions of integrity. Explain that having integrity is doing the right thing and staying strong, even when life gets tough or people doubt you.

◉ INTEGRITY: being honest and doing the right thing, even when no one is watching

Introduce Proverbs 10:9: "Whoever walks in integrity walks securely, but he who makes his ways crooked will be found out." Ask students to discuss this verse and how it relates to integrity. Explain that today's lesson and the story of Job will focus on the importance of staying strong and keeping your personal values when life gets tough.

3. Bible story:

Read and discuss the story of Job in the Book of Job. Focus on key passages: Job 1:1, 1:20-22, 2:9-10, and 42:10-17. Job was a righteous man who lived his life in a way that pleased God. But many bad things happened to him - he lost his wealth, his children, and even his health. Despite his friends telling him to curse God, and the trials he went through, Job never lost faith in God.

4. Activities:

* Bible story: The tale of Job
* Bible quiz: The story of Job
* Bible word search puzzle: The righteous man's trials
* Worksheet: What's the Word?
* Bible verse coloring page: Proverbs 10:9
* Worksheet: Walking in integrity
* Creative writing: The integrity of Job

The tale of Job

In a place called Uz, there lived a man named Job. He was a man who was known for always doing the right thing before God. He was rich, had a big family, and was healthy. Because of all this, he was known as the greatest man in the east. Job's sons loved to throw parties at their houses. They would take turns hosting and always invite their sisters to join them for good food and drinks. When their parties were over, Job would wake up early in the morning to pray for his children.

However, one day, many bad things started happening to Job. He lost all his money and animals, his children died in a terrible accident, and he got sick with painful sores all over his body. Despite all this, Job never stopped believing in God and doing what was right. His friends came to visit and told him that he must have done something wrong to deserve all these troubles.

Job knew he hadn't done anything wrong. While he didn't understand why all these terrible things were happening to him, he trusted that God had a plan. After a long time of hardship and pain, life finally began to change. God healed him from his sickness and gave him back more than he had before - twice as many animals, and even more children! After this, he lived 140 years and saw his sons and grandsons, four generations. And Job died an old man, and full of days.

The story OF JOB

Read Job 1:1-2:13 and 41:1-42:17. Answer the questions below.

1. In which land did Job and his family live?

2. Before his trials, how many children did Job have?

3. How did Job's children die?

4. What did God say to Satan (the adversary) about Job?

5. Who encouraged Job to curse God?

6. When Job's friends arrived, how long did they sit in silence?

7. What did Job's friends give him?

8. From where did God answer Job?

9. Where did the Leviathan live?

10. After Job repented, what did God do for him?

The righteous MAN'S TRIALS

Read Job 1:1-2:13.
Find and circle each of the words from the list below.

B	B	O	J	Q	U	P	R	I	G	H	T	L	T	E
Y	Y	I	L	W	A	Y	E	A	Z	S	S	J	E	W
S	A	K	Z	R	H	J	I	X	U	I	G	L	N	Z
R	I	S	K	M	S	K	B	H	F	L	R	Z	C	K
Z	D	Z	H	Q	B	D	Y	E	K	S	E	T	H	Z
K	R	V	O	E	A	U	P	Y	A	A	A	P	I	B
O	G	L	W	P	S	W	K	N	X	T	T	C	L	L
S	E	R	V	A	N	T	P	Y	U	A	W	O	D	A
C	H	A	L	D	E	A	N	S	M	N	I	H	R	M
Z	B	A	R	I	F	S	M	Z	F	Q	N	E	E	E
L	V	D	P	U	I	B	I	J	V	V	D	D	N	L
O	G	G	Q	Z	X	Q	E	E	E	M	B	G	F	E
N	A	D	V	E	R	S	I	T	Y	D	K	E	C	S
J	W	B	S	U	F	F	E	R	I	N	G	V	D	S
F	Z	P	O	S	S	E	S	S	I	O	N	S	P	K

SATAN

ASHES

UPRIGHT

TEN CHILDREN

HEDGE

ADVERSITY

CHALDEANS

BLAMELESS

POSSESSIONS

GREAT WIND

SUFFERING

SERVANT

What's the Word?

Read Job 2:1-10 (ESV). Using the words below,
fill in the blanks to complete the Bible passage.

SATAN	JOB	INTEGRITY	WOMEN	BLAMELESS
SERVANT	POTTERY	ASHES	FOOT	DESTROY

" There was a day when the sons of God came to present themselves before Him, and Satan also came among them to present himself before God. And God said to Satan, "From where have you come?" Satan answered God and said, "From going to and fro on the earth, and from walking up and down on it." God said to ...., "Have you considered my .... Job, that there is none like him on the earth, a .... and upright man, who fears God and turns away from evil? He still holds fast his ...., although you incited me against him to .... him without reason." Satan answered God and said, "Skin for skin! All that a man has he will give for his life. But stretch out your hand and touch his bone and his flesh, and he will curse you to your face." God said to Satan, "Behold, he is in your hand; only spare his life." So, Satan went out from the presence of God and struck .... with loathsome sores from the sole of his .... to the crown of his head. And he took a piece of broken .... with which to scrape himself while he sat in the .... Then his wife said to him, "Do you still hold fast your integrity? Curse God and die." But he said to her, "You speak as one of the foolish .... would speak. Shall we receive good from God, and shall we not receive evil?" In all this Job did not sin with his lips. "

"Whoever walks in integrity walks securely, but he who makes his ways crooked will be found out."

(Proverbs 10:9)

Walking in integrity

Memorize Proverbs 10:9:

"Whoever walks in integrity walks securely,
but he who makes his ways crooked will be found out."
Write it down two times to help you remember.

Walking in integrity like Job did means always choosing to do what's right, even when no one else is looking!

Read the story of Job. Answer the questions:

How did God test Job's integrity?

....

How did Job keep his integrity and faith in God?

....

When you experience a difficult situation, how do you stand strong in your faith?

....

Connect to your life:

Think of a time when you chose to do the right thing, even when no one was watching (just like Job). Write about it.

....

....

Bible word unscramble:

Unscramble the letters to form words that relate to the story of Job.

NITRGETIY (Hint: Another word for always doing what's right) ....

OJB (Hint: The name of the man in our story) ....

IHTFA (Hint: Belief in God) ....

SSLEBINGS (Hint: Good things given by God) ....

The integrity of Job

Read the story of Job in the Book of Job.
Using the vocabulary below, rewrite this story in your own words.

....

....

....

....

....

....

....

....

....

....

....

....

JOB	CHILDREN
CURSE	FRIENDS
GOD	WIFE

COMPASSION

Proverbs 14:21 and the story of Feeding the 5000

1. Lesson objectives:

Students will be able to explain the key message of Proverbs 14:21, define compassion, and retell the story of Feeding the 5000 and what it reveals about kindness to one's neighbors.

2. Introduction:

Begin the lesson by introducing the concept of compassion. Ask students to offer their definitions of compassion. Explain that having compassion lets you understand and feel what someone else is going through, and wanting to help or be kind to them. Whenever you see someone in need and you offer a helping hand or a kind word, that's compassion in action.

◉ COMPASSION: a feeling of sympathy or concern for the suffering of others, and a wish to help them

Introduce Proverbs 14:21: "Whoever despises his neighbor is a sinner, but blessed is he who is generous to the poor." Ask students to discuss this verse and how it relates to compassion. Explain that today's lesson and the Bible story of Feeding the 5000 will focus on how our Messiah showed compassion to others.

3. Bible story:

Read and discuss the story of Feeding the 5000 in John 6:1-14 and Matthew 14:13-21. Yeshua, while teaching a crowd of about 5000 people, saw they were hungry and had no food. His disciples suggested sending the crowd away to find food, but Yeshua fed them with just five loaves of bread and two fish, brought by a young boy. Everyone ate and was satisfied, and there were even 12 baskets of leftovers.

4. Activities:

* Bible story: Five loaves, two fish
* Bible quiz: Feeding the 5000
* Bible word search puzzle: Feeding the 5000
* Worksheet: What's the Word?
* Bible verse coloring page: John 6:9
* Worksheet: Showing compassion
* Creative writing: Compassion in action

Five loaves, two fish

Yeshua and His disciples traveled to the other side of the Sea of Galilee, also known as the Sea of Tiberias. While they were up on a mountain, Yeshua saw a large crowd of people coming towards Him. Yeshua turned to one of His disciples, Philip, and asked, "Where can we buy bread so these people can eat?" He asked this not because He didn't know what to do, but to see what Philip would say.

Philip answered, "Even if we had 200 denarii worth of bread, it wouldn't be enough for everyone to have a little bite." Another disciple, Andrew, pointed out a boy who had five loaves of bread and two fish. But, he wondered, "How far can that go among so many people?"

Yeshua told everyone to sit down on the grassy mountain. Then, taking the five loaves and two fish, gave thanks, and distributed them to the people. Everyone ate as much as they wanted. After everyone was full, Yeshua told His disciples, "Gather all the leftover pieces so nothing is wasted." They gathered everything and filled twelve baskets with leftovers. The crowd could hardly believe their eyes. "This must be the Prophet who is to come into the world!" they cried.

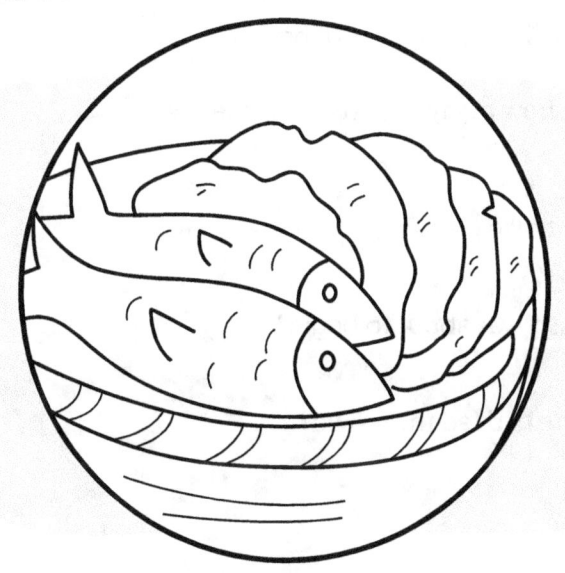

Feeding the 5000

Read John 6:1-15. Answer the questions below

1. What food did a young boy have with him?

2. How many people gathered to hear Yeshua teach?

3. What is another name for the Sea of Galilee?

4. In which place were Yeshua and His disciples when He fed the people?

5. Why did Yeshua ask Philip, "Where shall we buy bread for the people to eat?

6. What did Yeshua do when He held the loaves of bread?

7. After the people had eaten, how many baskets were filled with fragment of bread?

8. In what region did this event take place?

9. Which Appointed Time (Feast) was about to begin?

10. Where did Yeshua go after he had fed the crowd?

Feeding the 5000

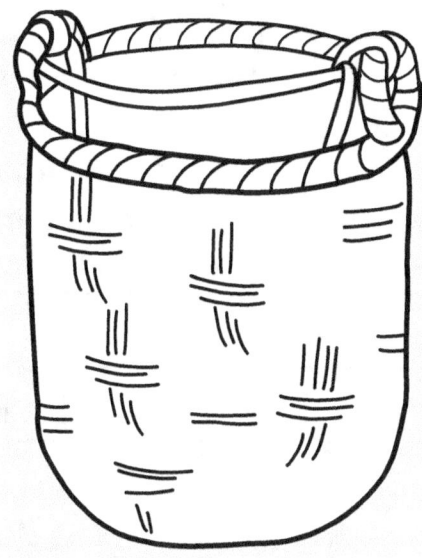

Read John 6:1-15. Find and circle the words below.

T	H	I	G	U	S	W	H	S	F	C	B	O	X	F
S	E	B	P	E	F	Z	P	K	I	X	A	J	K	T
S	Q	A	J	F	F	O	B	W	U	Q	R	U	P	W
I	V	A	C	F	B	C	Y	R	Q	K	L	Q	A	F
L	A	F	D	H	J	N	D	Y	E	D	E	D	S	I
Z	P	L	H	W	G	V	F	W	W	A	Y	T	S	S
O	D	R	F	O	D	O	L	O	D	J	D	I	O	H
L	A	N	D	O	F	I	S	R	A	E	L	B	V	E
W	S	L	X	C	H	I	R	F	O	Q	H	E	E	R
Q	P	H	I	L	I	P	I	O	I	F	R	R	R	M
S	O	Z	B	J	Y	L	T	O	Z	S	D	I	H	A
O	S	D	I	S	C	I	P	L	E	S	H	A	Y	N
J	F	G	P	E	O	O	Q	R	S	P	M	S	R	F
M	U	N	L	E	A	V	E	N	E	D	Y	T	H	C
G	A	L	I	L	E	E	T	I	K	G	T	R	B	K

PASSOVER

PHILIP

BREAD

FISHERMAN

TEACH

FISH

GALILEE

UNLEAVENED

LAND OF ISRAEL

DISCIPLES

TIBERIAS

BARLEY

What's the Word?

Read Matthew 14:13-21 (ESV). Using the words below,
fill in the blanks to complete the Bible passage.

BOAT	FISH	COMPASSION	BASKETS	HEAVEN
CROWDS	DISCIPLES	LOAVES	FOOD	VILLAGES

" Now when Yeshua heard this, He withdrew from there in a .... to a desolate

place by Himself. But when the .... heard it, they followed Him on foot from

the towns. When He went ashore He saw a great crowd, and He had ....

on them and healed their sick. Now when it was evening, the .... came

to Him and said, "This is a desolate place, and the day is now over; send the crowds

away to go into the .... and buy .... for themselves." But Yeshua

said, "They need not go away; you give them something to eat." They said to Him, "We

have only five .... here and two fish." And He said, "Bring them here to Me."

Then He ordered the crowds to sit down on the grass, and taking the five loaves and

the two ...., He looked up to .... and said a blessing. Then He

broke the loaves and gave them to the disciples, and the disciples gave them to the

crowds. And they all ate and were satisfied. And they took up twelve

.... full of the broken pieces left over. And those

who ate were about five thousand men, besides

women and children. "

There is a boy
HERE WHO
has five loaves
and two fish...
(JOHN 6:9)

www.biblepathwayadventures.com
Bible Proverbs for Kids Activity Book

Showing compassion

How would you describe Yeshua's character?

....
....
....
....
....
....
....
....

How did Yeshua show compassion in this story?

....
....
....
....
....
....
....
....

How do you think the people felt when Yeshua fed them?

....
....
....
....
....
....

Draw a picture to retell the story of Feeding the 5000.

Compassion in action

Read the story of Feeding the 5000 in John 6:1-15.
Using the vocabulary below, rewrite this story in your own words.

....
....
....
....
....
....
....
....
....
....
....
....

FISH	CROWD
BREAD	PASSOVER
DISCIPLES	DENARII

RESPONSIBILITY

Proverbs 27:23 and the story of Noah's ark

1. Lesson objectives:

Students will be able to explain the key message of Proverbs 27:23, define responsibility, and discuss how the story of Noah builds an ark shows that responsibility includes not just tasks and chores, but also caring for others.

2. Introduction:

Begin the lesson by introducing the concept of responsibility. Ask students to offer their definitions of responsibility. Explain that being responsible means taking charge of your actions and understanding that what you do (or don't do) can affect others.

◎ RESPONSIBILITY: something that is your job or duty to deal with

Introduce Proverbs 27:23: "Know well the condition of your flocks and give attention to your herds." Ask students to discuss this verse and how it relates to responsibility. Explain that today's lesson will focus on the Bible story of Noah's ark, a tale of obedience, faith and great responsibility.

3. Bible story:

Read and discuss the story of Noah builds an ark in Genesis 6:1-22. Seeing the wickedness on earth, God decided to destroy mankind with a flood, sparing only Noah and his family. Before he did this, He gave Noah a very responsible job. He told Noah to build a gigantic ark and bring both clean and unclean animals into it, along with enough food for everyone to survive a great flood. And Noah obeyed God.

4. Activities:

* Bible story: Noah builds an ark
* Bible quiz: Noah builds an ark
* Bible word search puzzle: Noah's ark
* Worksheet: What's the Word?
* Bible verse coloring page: Proverbs 27:23
* Worksheet: Embracing responsibility
* Creative writing: Faith and responsibility

Noah builds an ark

Noah was a righteous man who walked with God. But he was different to other people. He tried to live his life in a way that pleased God. But others at that time did not pay attention to God's ways. They were continually wicked, and the earth was filled with violence. God regretted that He had made man on earth. He said to Noah, "I've decided to destroy all living beings, for they have filled the earth with violence. I will wipe everything out and start again."

Noah couldn't believe his ears. God was going to destroy everything? He told himself that God must think the earth was pretty wicked. But God had more to say. "Prepare an ark using gopher wood. Make rooms within it and coat it thoroughly with pitch, both inside and out. The ark will be 300 cubits long, 50 cubits wide, and 30 cubits high. Build a roof for the ark, leaving a cubit space to its top, and place the door on its side. Build three levels: lower, middle, and upper. I will send a great flood to wipe out every person and animal on earth."

God made a special promise, or 'covenant', with Noah. Noah and his family would be safe inside the ark. He said, "I will uphold my promise to you. You, along with your sons, your wife, and your sons' wives, shall come into the ark. You will also bring pairs of every living creature, male and female, into the ark to preserve their lives. Take with you seven pairs of all clean animals and one pair of unclean animals. And take with you every sort of food and store it inside the ark." God gave Noah great responsibility, and Noah did as he was instructed; he carried out all of God's instructions.

Noah builds AN ARK

Read Genesis 6:1-22. Answer the questions below.

① Who were the mighty men of renown?

② Noah was a _____ man, blameless in his generation.

③ Why did God regret making man on earth?

④ Who were Noah's sons?

⑤ What did God tell Noah to build?

⑥ How big was the ark that Noah built?

⑦ How many windows did the ark have?

⑧ How many decks did the ark have?

⑨ How did God plan to destroy everything on earth?

⑩ With whom did God say He would establish His covenant?

Noah's ARK

Read Genesis 6:1-8:12. Find and circle the words below.

```
N I B R A R L Z V Z A Y I Q X
C W X O A P A F S K A U W A U
W L P S L L T I Q J G J U N T
G T E Z W I T P N T O Q G O B
V I J A Y H V A R B O A A A P
O A J G N F Q E R Z O Z Q H D
F L O O D A H D L Z L W Z I W
K G W F P A N C U E X G W S Z
D U Q E D D A I I H A B A M G
T S W I N D O W M U H F T G P
K W N O N A R L P A C Y E Y I
G X P U V C I J G K L T R D T
C D R C O V E N A N T S O O C
O Y X S A Y X W B P M Q A Y H
U N C L E A N A N I M A L S I
```

WINDOW

ANIMALS

RAINBOW

FLOOD

ALTAR

PITCH

NOAH

COVENANT

WATER

UNCLEAN ANIMALS

OLIVE LEAF

CLEAN ANIMALS

What's the Word?

Read Genesis 6:1-22 (ESV). Using the words below,
fill in the blanks to complete the Bible passage.

ARK	NOAH	FLOOD	FEMALE	CUBITS
LIVING	WATERS	COVENANT	FOOD	ANIMALS

" "Make yourself an .... of gopher wood. Make rooms in the ark, and cover it inside and out with pitch. This is how you are to make it: the length of the ark 300 ...., its breadth 50 cubits, and its height 30 cubits. Make a roof for the ark, and finish it to a cubit above, and set the door of the ark in its side. Make it with lower, second, and third decks. For behold, I will bring a .... of .... upon the earth to destroy all flesh in which is the breath of life under heaven. Everything that is on the earth shall die. But I will establish my .... with you, and you shall come into the ark, you, your sons, your wife, and your sons' wives with you. And of every .... thing of all flesh, you shall bring two of every sort into the ark to keep them alive with you. They shall be male and .... Of the birds according to their kinds, and of the .... according to their kinds, of every creeping thing of the ground, according to its kind, two of every sort shall come in to you to keep them alive. Also take with you every sort of food that is eaten, and store it up. It shall serve as .... for you and for them." .... did this; he did all that God commanded him. "

"Know well the condition of your flocks and give attention to your herds."

(Proverbs 27:23)

Embracing responsibility

Read Proverbs 27:23:

"Know well the condition of your flocks and give attention to your herds."
What do you think this verse is trying to tell you about responsibility?

....

Read and reflect:

Read the story of Noah's ark in Genesis 6:1–7:16. List three ways that Noah
showed responsibility in this Bible passage.

....

....

....

Responsibility in practice:

Can you think of a time when you showed responsibility like Noah? Write a
short paragraph about it below.

....

....

God gave Noah great responsibility. Draw an example of this. Remember to
include the animals!

Faith and responsibility

Read the story of Noah builds an ark in Genesis 6:1-22.
Using the vocabulary below, rewrite this story in your own words.

....
....
....
....
....
....
....
....
....
....
....

NOAH	CLEAN
NEPHILIM	CUBITS
ARK	ANIMALS

SELF-CONTROL

Proverbs 25:28 and the story of David and King Saul

1. Lesson objectives:

Students will be able to explain the key message of Proverbs 25:28, define self-control, and understand the benefits of self-control through the story of David spares King Saul.

2. Introduction:

Begin the lesson by introducing the concept of self-control. Ask students to offer their definitions of self-control. Explain that self-control is like having an inner brake system. Even when you really want to do something, you think about whether it's a good idea and decide what's best for you and others around you. It's a skill that helps you be in charge of your actions, even when things get tough or tempting.

◎ SELF-CONTROL: the ability to control your emotions and actions

Introduce Proverbs 25:28: "A man without self-control is like a city broken into and left without walls." Ask students to discuss this verse and how it relates to self-control. Explain that today's lesson will focus on the Bible story of David spares King Saul, and how demonstrating self-control in our daily life can please God.

3. Bible story:

Read and discuss the story of David and King Saul in 1 Samuel 24:1-22. David had the chance to kill King Saul, who was pursuing him to take his life. But instead, he merely cut off a corner of Saul's robe to prove he did not mean to hurt him. David's act of self-control convinced Saul that David was righteous and unwilling to harm God's anointed.

4. Activities:

* Bible story: A king spared
* Bible quiz: David spares Saul's life
* Bible word search puzzle: David spares Saul's life
* Worksheet: What's the Word?
* Bible verse coloring page: Proverbs 25:28
* Worksheet: Self-control superheroes!
* Creative writing: Mercy in the wilderness

A king spared

After chasing the Philistines, King Saul heard that David was hiding in the wilderness of Engedi. He took 3000 men and went to find him. On the way, he needed to use the bathroom and went into a cave where David and his men were hiding. David's men said to him, "This is the day God spoke of when He said, 'Behold, I will give your enemy into your hand!'"

David crept up to King Saul and cut off a piece of his robe. Afterwards, he felt guilty for harming the king. He said to his men, "I cannot hurt God's anointed one. Do not attack him." And so, King Saul safely left the cave. A short time later, David came out of the cave and called out to him, saying, "Why do you listen to others who want to harm me? Today, God gave you into my hands, but I spared you. I won't harm you, even though you want to kill me."

King Saul answered, "You are more righteous than me. You have repaid me good, whereas I have repaid you evil. God will reward you for your kindness. Promise me you won't hurt my family when you become king." Then the king returned home while David and his men went on their way.

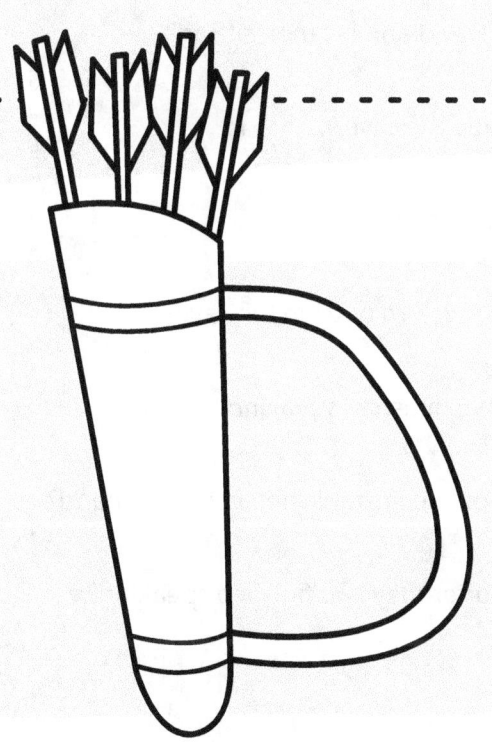

David spares
SAUL'S LIFE

Read 1 Samuel 24:1-22. Answer the questions below.

1. Where had Saul returned from?

2. How many men did Saul choose to help him find David?

3. Why did Saul go into the cave?

4. In what part of the cave were David and his men sitting?

5. What did David do to Saul inside the cave?

6. What did David forbid his men to do?

7. What did David do when Saul saw him outside the cave?

8. What did Saul do after David had finished speaking?

9. What kingdom did Saul say would be established in David's hand?

10. Where did Saul and David go after they had finished speaking?

David spares SAUL'S LIFE

Read 1 Samuel 24:1-22. Find and circle the words below.

```
H E B R E W O C Z W R I Z C C
S V T A S S E L S M O S N D S
E S U U H E Y G C U B R H R X
L E O J L F N H O D E A K E A
F O X L O H U H N R X E U N L
C I T P D H T Y V O G L U G M
O W F H O I U J M C I I Z E D
N K E X Q H E Y W K R T G D A
T V C I G J I R F P Z E F I V
R R O D I P T N K V Y T X G I
O M D K I N G D O M G G E Q D
L M W Z F L W T D K Y M R I B
H I L Q R X A P Y Z B I X Y P
J A G S K I N G S A U L P W J
A N O I N T E D H N L C V G J
```

HEBREW

KINGDOM

ROCK

ENGEDI

TASSELS

SOLDIER

ISRAELITE

ANOINTED

ROBE

KING SAUL

SELF-CONTROL

DAVID

What's the Word?

Read 1 Samuel 24:1-7 (ESV). Using the words below,
fill in the blanks to complete the Bible passage.

PHILISTINES	DAVID	ROBE	MEN
GOD	CAVE	ANOINTED	ISRAEL

" When Saul returned from following the ...., he was told, "Behold, David is in the wilderness of Engedi." Saul took three thousand chosen men out of all .... and went to find .... and his men in front of the Wild goats' Rocks. He came to the sheepfolds where there was a ...., and went in to relieve himself. Now David and his men were sitting in the innermost parts of the cave. And David's men said to him, "Here is the day of which .... said to you, 'Behold, I will give your enemy into your hand, and you shall do to him as it shall seem good to you.'" Then David arose and stealthily cut off a corner of Saul's .... But afterwards, David's heart struck him because he had cut off a corner of Saul's robe. He said to his men, "God forbid that I should do this thing to my lord, who is God's ...., to put my hand against him, seeing he is God's anointed." David persuaded his .... with these words and did not permit them to attack Saul. And Saul left the cave and went on his way. "

"A man without Self-control is like a city broken into and left without walls."

(Proverbs 25:28)

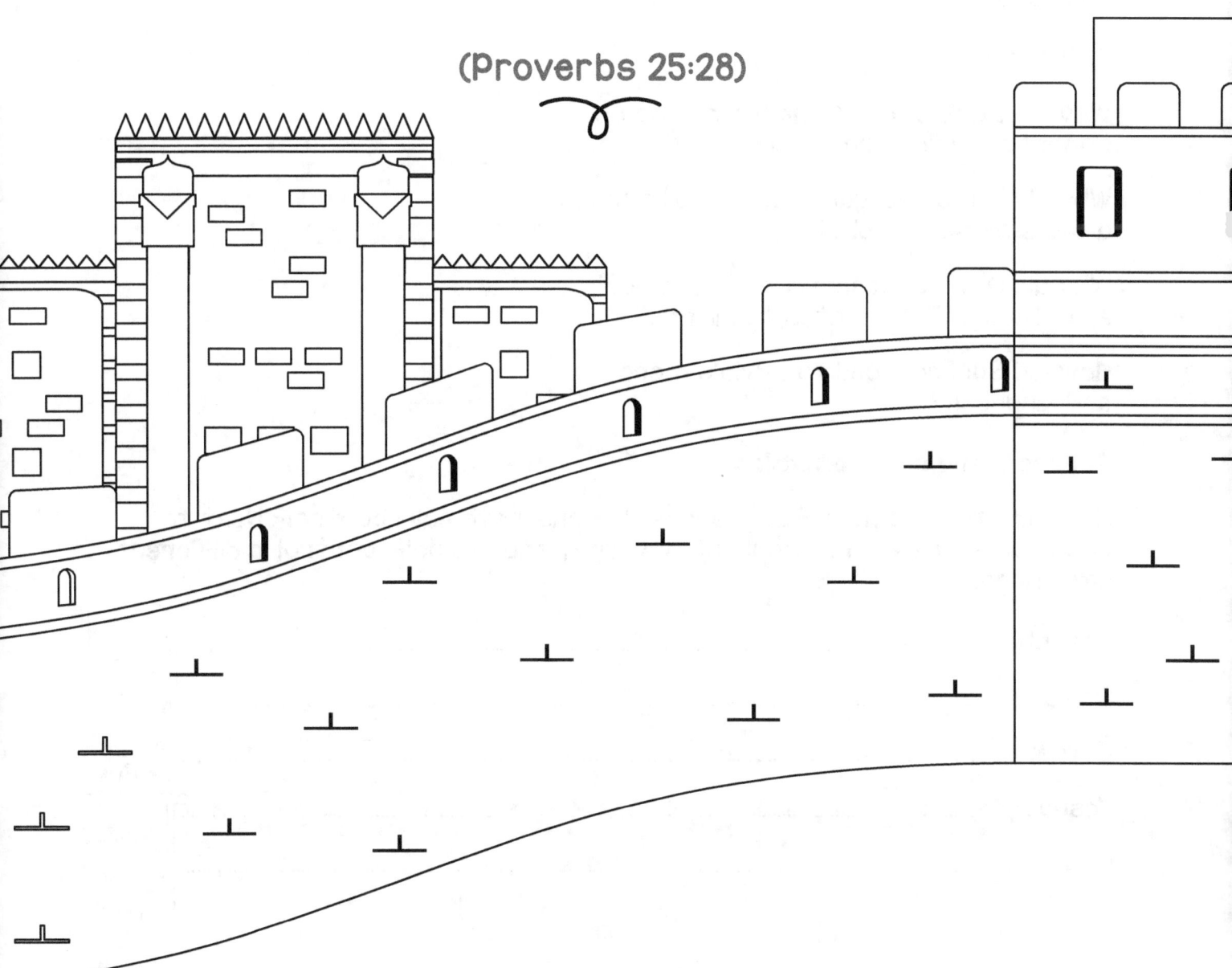

Self-control superheroes!

Self-control means making wise choices and controlling our actions, even in tough situations. Just like David, let's have self-control in our own lives. Read 1 Samuel 24:1-22. Complete the worksheet below.

1. The cave encounter:

Draw a picture of King Saul and David in the cave.

2. Questions:

Why did David's men think it was the perfect opportunity to harm Saul?

Why did David feel guilty after cutting off a piece of Saul's robe?

Why did David choose not to harm Saul, even though Saul wanted to kill him?

How did Saul respond to David's mercy and kindness?

3. Practising self-control:

How did other famous Bible heroes demonstrate self-control? Next to each name, write an example of how they showed self-control in different situations.

Joseph: ....

Daniel: ....

Esther: ....

Yeshua: ....

Paul: ....

BENJAMIN

JUDAH

Mercy in the wilderness

Read the story of David spares King Saul in 1 Samuel 24:1-22.
Using the vocabulary below, rewrite this story in your own words.

....
....
....
....
....
....
....
....
....
....
....

DAVID	CAVE
SAUL	ISRAEL
ROBE	RIGHTEOUS

DILIGENCE

Proverbs 21:5 and the story of Elijah and Elisha

1. Lesson objectives:

Students will be able to explain the key message of Proverbs 21:5, define diligence, and understand the importance of staying committed to whatever God has called you through the story of Elijah and Elisha.

2. Introduction:

Begin the lesson by introducing the concept of diligence. Ask students to offer their definitions of diligence. Explain that diligence is like being a determined detective or a focused builder. It means sticking to a task, doing it with care, and not giving up, even when things get tough. It's about putting in that extra effort to make sure things are done well.

◉ DILIGENCE: careful and persistent work or effort

Introduce Proverbs 21:5: "The plans of the diligent lead surely to abundance, but everyone who is hasty comes only to poverty." Ask students to discuss this verse and why staying committed to any task is important. Explain that today's lesson and the Bible story of Elijah and Elisha will focus the importance of staying diligent in a way that is pleasing to God.

3. Bible story:

Read and discuss the story of Elijah and Elisha in 2 Kings 2:1-15. As the moment approached for God to take the prophet Elijah to heaven in a whirlwind, his disciple Elisha refused to leave him, even though Elijah suggested it many times. When Elijah was swept into heaven by a flaming chariot, Elisha picked up his teacher's cloak and was given double the spiritual power that Elijah had.

4. Activities:

* Bible story: Elijah taken to Heaven
* Bible quiz: Elijah & Elisha
* Bible word search puzzle: Elijah taken to Heaven
* Worksheet: What's the Word?
* Bible verse coloring page: Proverbs 21:5
* Worksheet: Walking the extra mile
* Creative writing: Elijah's fiery departure

Elijah taken to Heaven

The prophet Elijah and his loyal disciple, Elisha, set off from Gilgal. God was readying to take Elijah to heaven via a whirlwind, and Elijah tried to encourage Elisha to stay back. "Stay here," he said. "God needs me to go to Bethel." Elisha replied, "As God lives and you live, I won't leave you!" So, together they journeyed to Bethel.

At Bethel, a group of local prophets approached Elisha. "Do you know that God will take your teacher away?" Elisha answered, "Yes, I know. Keep quiet." Again, Elijah turned to Elisha and said, "Stay here. God has commanded me to go to Jericho." But Elisha replied, "As long as God and you live, I won't leave you." So, together they journeyed to Jericho.

A group of prophets in Jericho came to Elisha and said, "Do you know that God will take your teacher away?" Again, Elisha replied, "Yes, I know. Be quiet." Once more, Elijah tried to stop Elisha from following him, this time to the Jordan River. But Elisha vowed not to leave him. When they reached the Jordan, Elijah rolled up his cloak and struck the river, parting the waters and they crossed on dry land. On the other side, Elijah, knowing he would soon leave, asked Elisha what he wanted before he departed. Elisha requested a double portion of Elijah's spiritual power.

Elijah told him his request was difficult, but possible—if Elisha saw him being taken away. And so, it happened. A fiery chariot with flaming horses swept in and separated them, whisking Elijah into the whirlwind towards heaven. Picking up Elijah's fallen cloak, Elisha knew he had gained the double portion of his teacher's spirit.

Elijah & ELISHA

Read 2 Kings 2:1-15. Answer the questions below.

1. From which place did Elijah and Elisha start their journey?

2. Where did Elijah tell Elisha God was sending him first?

3. How did Elisha respond each time Elijah asked him to stay behind?

4. Who warned Elisha that God would take Elijah from him?

5. What did Elijah use to part the waters of the Jordan River?

6. Before Elijah was taken to heaven, what did Elisha ask from him?

7. How was Elijah taken up to heaven?

8. What did Elisha do when he realized Elijah had been taken to heaven?

9. What miracle did Elisha perform at the Jordan River?

10. What did the sons of the prophets at Jericho do when they saw Elisha?

Elijah taken to HEAVEN

Read 2 Kings 2:1-15. Find and circle the words below.

```
C W Z Q E P M L D X Z R P M U
Z H W H I R L W I N D G R B K
C K A F Y J K D B F A S O F W
S N S R U G P D C D S D P G A
P I G S I E X Y P M H C H R T
I M R Z D O T M Y E E K E D E
R Y C C Z O T C L O A K T O R
I E L I S H A S C N V S S C D
T U T V P R U X O E E G W C B
G I L G A L Q C W F N Z N Y E
Q V A N A L A X C W F V V I T
N X K Q C W T J R D M I L T H
J O R D A N R I V E R A R B E
Q V X K U B S Y Q E D W A E L
A O B I J E L I J A H Q R I K
```

BETHEL

GILGAL

CLOAK

SPIRIT

WHIRLWIND

PROPHETS

ELIJAH

HEAVEN

ELISHA

CHARIOTS OF FIRE

JORDAN RIVER

WATER

What's the Word?

Read 2 Kings 2:2-11 (ESV). Using the words below,
fill in the blanks to complete the Bible passage.

WATER	JORDAN	CHARIOTS	MASTER	ELIJAH
ELISHA	WHIRLWIND	PROPHETS	JERICHO	PORTION

" Elijah said to Elisha, "Stay here, for God has sent me as far as Bethel." Elisha said, "As God lives, and as you live, I will not leave you." So they went down to Bethel. The sons of the prophets who were in Bethel came out to .... and said to him, "Do you know that today God will take away your .... from over you?" And he said, "Yes, I know it; keep quiet." Elijah said to him, "Elisha, please stay here, for God has sent me to ...." But he said, "As God lives, and as you yourself live, I will not leave you." So they came to Jericho. The sons of the prophets who were at Jericho drew near to Elisha and said to him, "Do you know that today God will take away your master from over you?" And he answered, "Yes, I know it; keep quiet." Then Elijah said to him, "Stay here, for God has sent me to the Jordan." But he said, "As God lives, and as you yourself live, I will not leave you." So the two of them went on. Fifty men of the sons of the .... also went and stood at some distance from them, as they both were standing by the .... Elijah took his cloak, rolled it up and struck the water. The .... was parted to the one side and to the other, till the two of them could go over on dry ground. When they had crossed, ... said to Elisha, "Ask what I shall do for you, before I am taken away." Elisha said, "Let there be a double .... of your spirit on me." And he said, "You have asked a hard thing; yet, if you see me as I am being taken from you, it shall be so for you. But if you do not see me, it shall not be so." As they still went on and talked, behold, ... and horses of fire separated the two of them. And Elijah went up by a .... into heaven. "

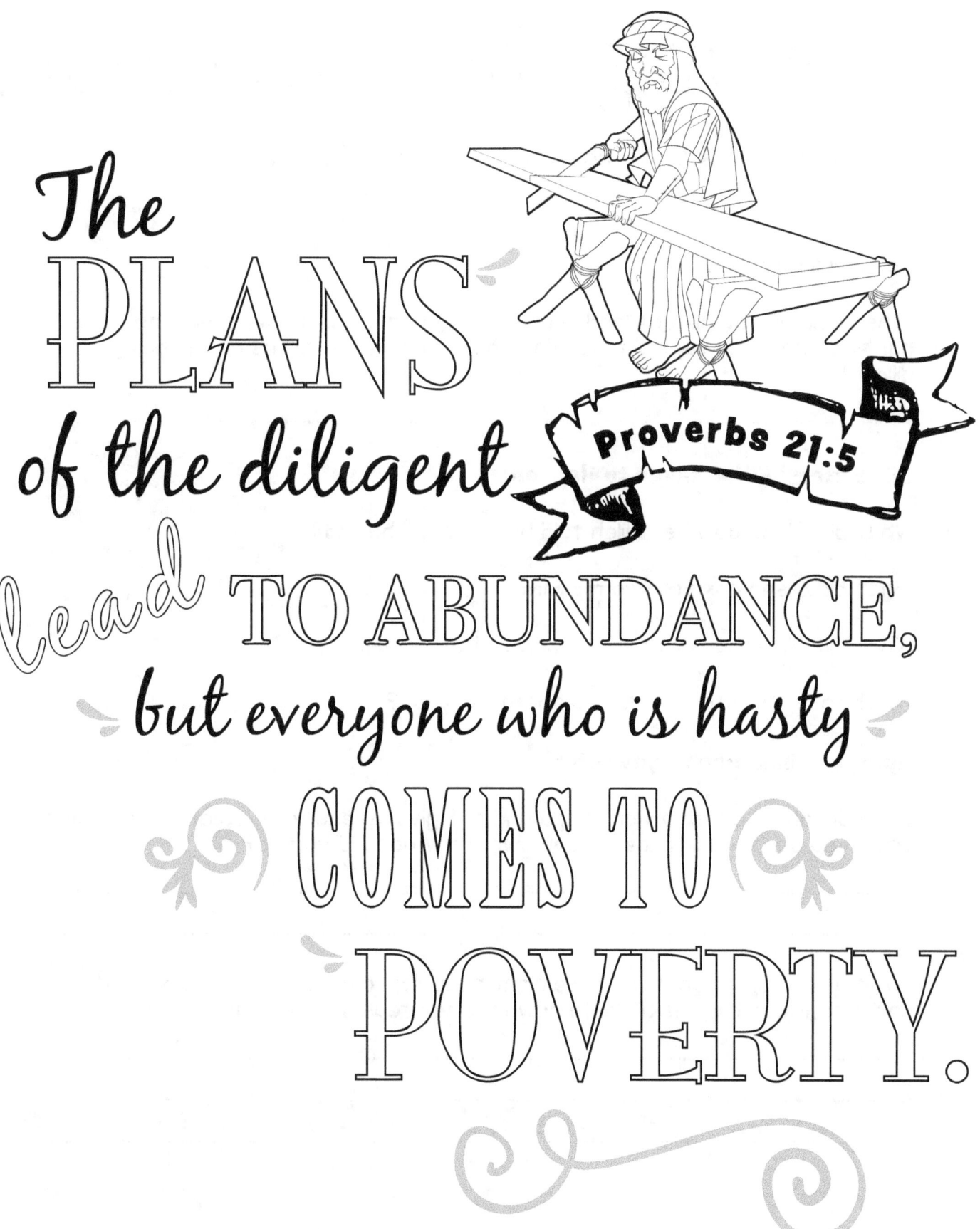

The
PLANS
of the diligent
Proverbs 21:5
lead TO ABUNDANCE,
but everyone who is hasty
COMES TO
POVERTY.

Walking the extra mile

Read 2 Kings 2:1-15 and Proverbs 21:5. Answer the questions below.

Read Proverbs 21:5:

"The plans of the diligent lead surely to abundance, but everyone who is hasty comes only to poverty." What does this verse tell us about being diligent?

....

Bible story: Elijah taken to Heaven:

What did Elisha do when Elijah told him to stay behind?

What did Elisha ask for from Elijah?

What did Elisha have to do to receive what he asked for?

What does this story teach us about diligence?

Applying diligence to your life:

Being diligent means to work hard and not give up easily. Write about a time when you showed diligence in your own life. What did you do?

....

....

Think of a task or goal you have right now. How can you stay committed until you finish the task? Write down three steps you can take.

1. ....

2. ....

3. ....

Elijah's fiery departure

Read the story of Elijah and Elisha in 2 Kings 2:1-15.
Using the vocabulary below, rewrite this story in your own words.

....
....
....
....
....
....
....
....
....
....
....

ELISHA	PROPHETS
ELIJAH	WHIRLWIND
JORDAN	CLOAK

RESILIENCE

Proverbs 24:16 and the story of Paul visits Lystra

1. Lesson objectives:

Students will be able to explain the key message of Proverbs 24:16, define resilience, and retell the story of Paul in Lystra and what it reveals about resilience.

2. Introduction:

Begin the lesson by introducing the concept of resilience. Ask students to offer their definitions of resilience. Explain that resilience is like having a superpower that helps you face life's challenges head-on, learn from them, and come back even stronger. Resilient people don't stay down for long; they get back up, learn from what happened, and keep going.

◎ RESILIENCE: to be happy or successful again after something difficult has happened.

Introduce Proverbs 24:16: "For the righteous falls seven times and rises again, but the wicked stumble in times of calamity." Ask students to discuss this verse and how it relates to resilience. Explain that today's lesson will focus on the Bible story of Paul in Lystra, and how he demonstrated resilience when faced with opposition to his Faith.

3. Bible story:

Read and discuss the story of Paul visits Lystra in Acts 14:8-20. In Lystra, Paul healed a man born lame, resulting in the crowds mistakenly saying that Paul and Barnabas as gods. When men from Antioch and Iconium turned the crowd against them, Paul was stoned and left for dead. Despite this attack, Paul demonstrated resilience, rising to return to the city a while later.

4. Activities:

* Bible story: Braving the stones
* Bible quiz: Paul and Barnabas visit Lystra
* Bible crossword puzzle: False gods!
* Worksheet: What's the Word?
* Map activity: A journey to Lystra
* Worksheet: Learning about resilience
* Creative writing: Triumph over trials

Braving the stones

In the city of Lystra, Paul met a man who had been unable to walk since birth. As Paul spoke, the man listened carefully, revealing a deep faith. Recognizing this faith, Paul said in a loud voice, "Stand upright on your feet." To the crowd's amazement, the man sprang up and began walking. The local people could hardly believe their eyes. "The gods have come down to us in the likeness of men!" they cried. Barnabas, they called Zeus, and Paul, Hermes, because he was the chief speaker.

A local priest of Zeus brought oxen and garlands to the gates and wanted to offer sacrifice with the crowds, But Paul and Barnabas stopped him, saying, "Men, why are you doing these things? We also are men, of like nature with you, and we bring you news that you should turn from these vain things to a living God, who made the heaven and the earth and the sea and all that is in them. In past generations He allowed all the nations to walk in their own ways. Yet He did not leave himself without witness, for he did good by giving you rains from heaven and fruitful seasons."

Despite their pleas, it was tough to stop the crowd from worshipping them. But things took a dark turn when some Jews from Antioch and Iconium turned the crowd against Paul, who was then stoned and dragged outside the city. Miraculously, surrounded by his disciples, Paul rose, resilient, and continued his journey to Derbe alongside Barnabas.

Paul & Barnabas
VISIT LYSTRA

Read Acts 14:8-20. Answer the questions below.

1. How long had the man been crippled?

2. What did Paul say to the crippled man?

3. What happened to the crippled man after Paul spoke to him?

4. What was the name of the false god that Paul was called?

5. What was the name of the false god that Barnabas was called?

6. Where was the temple of Zeus located?

7. How did Paul and Barnabas react to being honored as gods?

8. Who persuaded the crowds to stone Paul?

9. What happened when the disciples gathered around Paul after he was stoned by the crowd?

10. Which town did Paul and Barnabas travel to next?

False GODS!

Read Acts 14:8-20 (ESV). Complete the crossword puzzle below.

ACROSS

4) Paul looked him and seeing that he had _____ to be made well, said, "Stand upright on your feet."

5) "Even with these words they scarcely restrained the people from offering _____ to them."

7) "The priest of Zeus brought oxen and _____ to the gates and wanted to offer sacrifice with the crowds."

8) "Barnabas they called _____, and Paul, Hermes, because he was the chief speaker."

DOWN

1) "When Barnabas and Paul heard of it, they tore their _____ and rushed out into the crowd."

2) "When the _____ gathered about him, Paul rose up and entered the city…"

3) "Now at _____ there was a man sitting who could not use his feet."

6) "Jews came from Antioch and _____, and having persuaded the crowds, they stoned Paul and dragged him out of the city."

What's the Word?

Read Acts 14:11-20 (ESV). Using the words below,
fill in the blanks to complete the Bible passage.

PAUL	DISCIPLES	SACRIFICE	ANTIOCH	TEMPLE
PRIEST	HEAVEN	BARNABAS	GENERATIONS	STONED

" When the crowds saw what .... had done, they lifted up their voices, saying in Lycaonian, "The gods have come down to us in the likeness of men!" Barnabas they called Zeus, and Paul, Hermes, because he was the chief speaker. And the .... of Zeus, whose .... was at the entrance to the city, brought oxen and garlands to the gates and wanted to offer .... with the crowds. But when the apostles .... and Paul heard of it, they tore their garments and rushed out into the crowd, crying out, "Men, why are you doing these things? We also are men, of like nature with you, and we bring you good news, that you should turn from these vain things to a living God, who made the heaven and the earth and the sea and all that is in them. In past .... he allowed all the nations to walk in their own ways. Yet he did not leave himself without witness, for he did good by giving you rains from .... and fruitful seasons, satisfying your hearts with food and gladness." Even with these words they scarcely restrained the people from offering sacrifice to them. But Jews came from .... and Iconium, and having persuaded the crowds, they .... Paul and dragged him out of the city, supposing that he was dead. But when the .... gathered about him, he rose up and entered the city, and on the next day he went on with Barnabas to Derbe. "

Journey to Lystra

At the time of Paul, the city of Lystra was a city bustling with different cultures and people. Located on a trade route bridging the eastern and western parts of the Roman Empire, it was home to a mix of people, including Greeks, Romans, and Jews. Archaeological evidence shows that Lystra was an economically thriving city with a rich culture and beautiful buildings. Many temples and religious structures, including a shrine dedicated to Zeus, marked the city's landscape. Today, the site of ancient Lystra can be found 19 miles south of the city of Konya (Iconium in the New Testament), north of the village of Hatunsaray in Turkey.

Read Acts 13-14. Trace Paul and Barnabas' journey from Perga to Derbe.

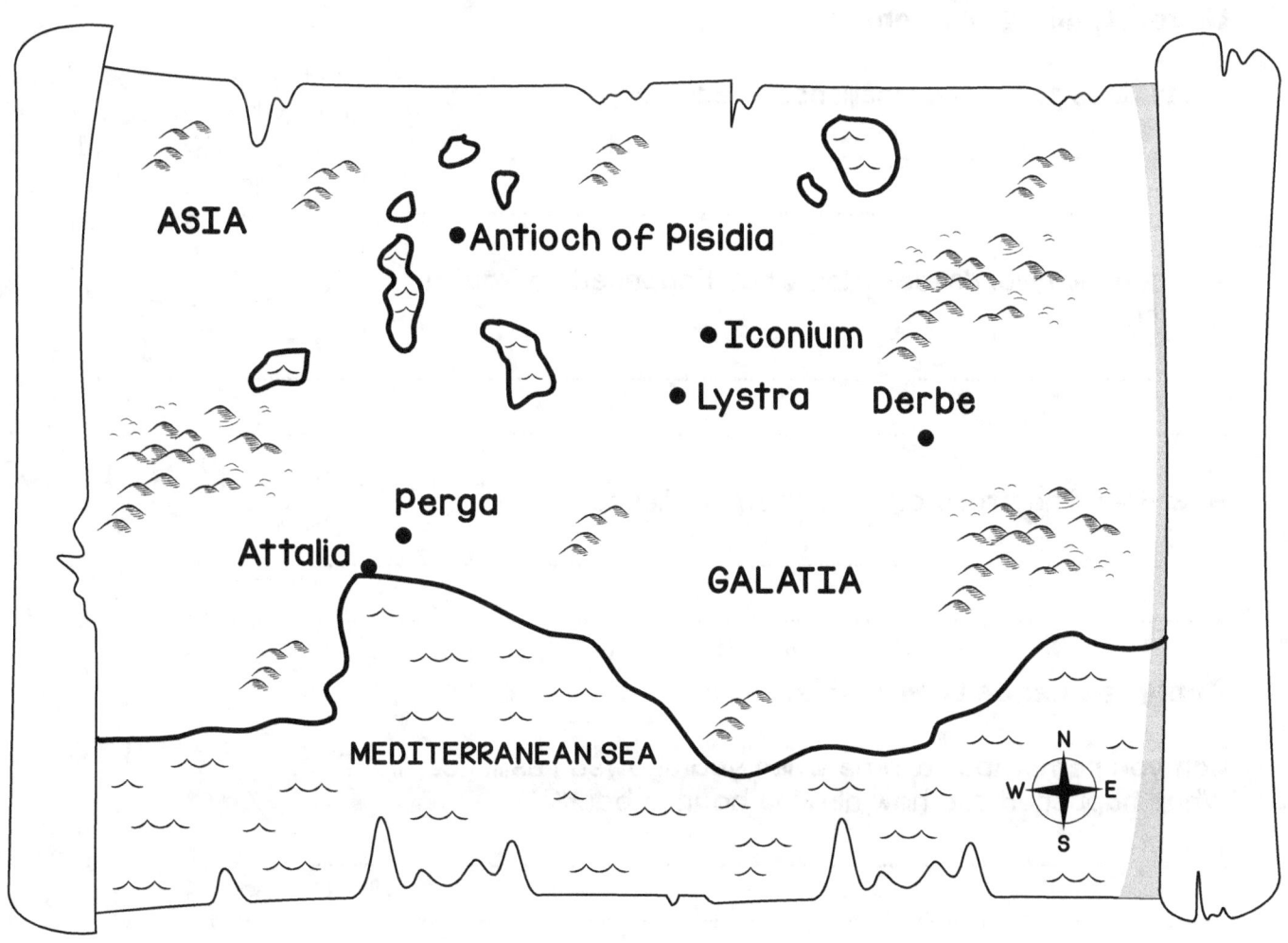

Learning about resilience

Read Acts 14:8-20 and Proverbs 24:16. Answer the questions below.

Read Proverbs 24:16:

"For the righteous falls seven times and rises again, but the wicked stumble in times of calamity." The story of Paul in Lystra talks about how Paul was mistaken for a god, and then attacked by the crowd. He showed great resilience by getting back up and continuing his mission. What does this proverb teach us about resilience?

....

Understanding resilience:

What does the word 'resilience' mean to you?

....

....

In your own words, describe what happened to Paul in Lystra.

> Just like in Proverbs 24:16 and Paul's story, we all can rise again when we fall or face challenges. That's what resilience is all about!

....

....

How does the story of Paul show resilience?

....

....

Apply resilience to your life:

Can you remember a time when you showed resilience, like Paul? What happened and how did you bounce back?

....

....

Triumph over trials

Read the story of Paul visits Lystra in Acts 14:8-20.
Using the vocabulary below, rewrite this story in your own words.

....

....

....

....

....

....

....

....

....

....

....

....

PAUL   ZEUS

BARNABAS   STONED

HERMES   LYSTRA

ANSWER KEY

HUMILITY
Bible quiz: Nebuchadnezzar restored

1. King Nebuchadnezzar was walking on the roof of the royal palace of Babylon
2. He claimed to have built the great Babylon by his mighty power as a royal residence and for the glory of his majesty
3. The voice said that the kingdom has departed from him, he shall be driven from among men, his dwelling shall be with the beasts of the field, and he will eat grass like an ox until he acknowledges that the Most High rules the kingdom of men
4. Seven periods of time
5. Nebuchadnezzar's hair grew as long as eagles' feathers, his body was wet with the dew of heaven, and his nails were like birds' claws
6. The king's reason returned to him, and he blessed and praised the Most High
7. The Most High, who lives forever and whose dominion is an everlasting dominion.
8. The glory of his kingdom, his majesty, and splendor returned to King Nebuchadnezzar
9. The king's counselors and his lords sought him
10. King Nebuchadnezzar learned that all the works of the King of heaven are right and his ways are just; and that the King of heaven is able to humble those who walk in pride

Bible word search puzzle: Nebuchadnezzar praises God

Worksheet: What's the Word?
All this came upon King Nebuchadnezzar. At the end of twelve months he was walking on the roof of the royal palace of Babylon, and the king answered and said, "Is not this great Babylon, which I have built by my mighty power as a royal residence and for the glory of my majesty?" While the words were still in the king's mouth, there fell a voice from heaven, "O King Nebuchadnezzar, to you it is spoken: The kingdom has departed from you, and you shall be driven from among men, and your dwelling shall be with the beasts of the field. And you shall be made to eat grass like an ox, and seven periods of time shall pass over you, until you know that the Most High rules the kingdom of men and gives it to whom he will." Immediately the word was fulfilled against Nebuchadnezzar. He was driven from among men and ate grass like an ox, and his body was wet with the dew of heaven till his hair grew as long as eagles' feathers, and his nails were like birds' claws.

FAITH
Bible quiz: David & Goliath

1. When David was young, he was a shepherd
2. The prophet Samuel anointed David as the next king of Israel
3. David played the harp / lyre
4. Valley of Elah
5. About 9 feet 9 inches
6. Forty days
7. King Saul gave David permission to fight Goliath
8. David picked five stones out of the stream
9. David hit Goliath with a stone from his sling
10. The Israelites celebrated David's great victory by singing and dancing, and playing instruments

Bible word search puzzle: David & Goliath

Worksheet: What's the Word?

David said to Goliath, "You come to me with a sword and with a spear and with a javelin, but I come to you in the name of the Lord of hosts, the God of the armies of Israel, whom you have defied. This day God will deliver you into my hand, and I will strike you down and cut off your head. I will give the dead bodies of the host of the Philistines this day to the birds of the air and to the wild beasts of the earth, that all the earth may know that there is a God in Israel, and that all this assembly may know that God saves not with sword and spear. For the battle is God's, and He will give you into our hand." When the Philistine arose and came and drew near to meet David, David ran quickly toward the battle line to meet the Philistine. And David put his hand in his bag and took out a stone and slung it and struck the Philistine on his forehead. The stone sank into his forehead, and he fell on his face to the ground. David prevailed over the Philistine with a sling and with a stone, and struck the Philistine and killed him. There was no sword in the hand of David.

GENEROSITY

Bible quiz: The widow's offering

1. Yeshua was teaching in the temple courts
2. Yeshua was watching the crowd putting their money into the temple treasury
3. Many rich people gave large amounts of money
4. A poor widow put in two very small copper coins
5. Yeshua said that the poor widow has put more into the treasury than all the others
6. The others gave out of their wealth, but the widow, out of her poverty, put in everything—all she had to live on
7. The widow's act of giving teaches us that the value of a gift is not determined by the amount, but by the generosity and sacrifice behind it
8. Ask children to answer this question. Answers may vary

Bible word search puzzle: The generous widow

Worksheet: What's the Word?

While Yeshua was teaching in the temple courts, he sat down opposite the place where the offerings were put and watched the crowd putting their money into the temple treasury. Many rich people threw in large amounts. But a poor widow came and put in two very small copper coins, worth only a few cents. Calling his disciples to him, Yeshua said, "Truly I tell you, this poor widow has put more into the treasury than all the others. They all gave out of their wealth; but she, out of her poverty, put in everything—all she had to live on."

KINDNESS

Bible quiz: The good Samaritan

1. A Torah teacher (lawyer)
2. "You shall love God with all your heart, soul, and strength; and your neighbor as yourself." (Deuteronomy 6:5)
3. The man was travelling to Jericho
4. He was robbed and beaten
5. A priest
6. A Levite
7. A Samaritan
8. Cleaned his wounds and paid an innkeeper to take care of him
9. Two denarii
10. The man who showed mercy on the injured traveler

Bible word search puzzle: The good Samaritan

Worksheet: What's the Word?

The Torah teacher, desiring to justify himself said to Yeshua, "Who is my neighbor?" Yeshua replied, "A man was going down from Jerusalem to Jericho and fell among robbers, who stripped him, beat him and departed, leaving him half dead. Now by chance a priest was going down that road, and when he saw him he passed by on the other side. Likewise, a Levite when he came to the place and saw him, passed by on the

other side. But a Samaritan, as he journeyed, came to where he was and when he saw him, he had compassion. He bound up his wounds, pouring on oil and wine. Then he set him on his own animal and brought him to an inn and took care of him. The next day he took out two denarii and gave them to the innkeeper, saying, 'Take care of him, and whatever more you spend I will repay you when I come back.' Which of these three do you think proved to be a neighbor to the man who fell among the robbers?" He said, "The one who showed him mercy." And Yeshua said to him, "Go and do likewise."

HONESTY
Bible quiz: Ananias & Sapphira
1. The early believers were described as being of one heart and soul, sharing everything in common
2. There was not a needy person among the believers, indicating that they took care of each other
3. The proceeds from the sold lands and houses were laid at the apostles' feet and distributed to each as they had need
4. Joseph, also known as Barnabas, was a Levite from Cyprus who sold a field and gave the money to the apostles
5. Ananias and Sapphira were a couple who sold a property, but kept part of the proceeds for themselves
6. After Peter confronted him, Ananias fell down and died
7. Sapphira came in about three hours after the death of Ananias
8. Sapphira confirmed the false amount that Ananias had given
9. Sapphira fell down at Peter's feet and died, just like her husband
10. The deaths of Ananias and Sapphira brought great fear upon the community and everyone who heard of the incidents

Bible word search puzzle: Divine judgment

Worksheet: What's the Word?
A man named Ananias and his wife Sapphira sold a piece of property, and with his wife's knowledge he kept back for himself some of the proceeds and brought only a part of it and laid it at the apostles' feet. Peter said, "Ananias, why has Satan filled your heart to lie to the Holy Spirit and to keep back for yourself part of the proceeds of the land? While it remained unsold, did it not remain your own? And after it was sold, was it not at your disposal? Why is it that you have contrived this deed in your heart? You have not lied to man but to God." When Ananias heard these words, he fell down and breathed his last. And great fear came upon all who heard of it. The young men rose and wrapped him up and carried him out and buried him. After an interval of about three hours his wife came in, not knowing what had happened. Peter said to her, "Tell me whether you sold the land for so much." And she said, "Yes, for so much." But Peter said to her, "How is it that you have agreed together to test the Spirit of God? Behold, the feet of those who have buried your husband are at the door, and they will carry you out." Immediately she fell down at his feet and breathed her last. When the young men came in they found her dead, and they carried her out and buried her beside her husband. And great fear came upon the whole church and upon all who heard of these things.

PATIENCE
Bible quiz: Abraham & Sarah
1. Abraham was sitting at the door of his tent near the oak trees of Mamre when he saw the three men
2. Abraham ran over to the three men and bowed down
3. Abraham offered to wash their feet, rest under the tree, and eat some bread
4. The three men were messengers of God
5. The promise made to Abraham was that Sarah would bear a son
6. Sarah was listening to the conversation from the tent
7. Sarah laughed to herself when she heard the promise, as she thought it was impossible due to her old age
8. God promised that Sarah would bear a son and this promise was to be fulfilled in a year's time
9. The son born to Abraham and Sarah was named Isaac
10. Abraham was a hundred years old when Isaac was born

Bible word search puzzle: Birth of Isaac

Worksheet: What's the Word?

Yahweh appeared to him by the oaks of Mamre, as he sat in the tent door in the heat of the day. He lifted up his eyes and looked, and saw that three men stood near him. When he saw them, he ran to meet them from the tent door, and bowed himself to the earth, and said, "My lord, if now I have found favor in your sight, please don't go away from your servant. Now let a little water be fetched, wash your feet, and rest yourselves under the tree. I will get a piece of bread so you can refresh your heart. After that you may go your way, now that you have come to your servant." They said, "Very well, do as you have said." Abraham hurried into the tent to Sarah, and said, "Quickly prepare three seahs of fine meal, knead it, and make cakes." Abraham ran to the herd, and fetched a tender and good calf, and gave it to the servant. He hurried to dress it. He took butter, milk, and the calf which he had dressed, and set it before them. He stood by them under the tree, and they ate. They asked him, "Where is Sarah, your wife?" He said, "There, in the tent." He said, "I will certainly return to you at about this time next year; and behold, Sarah your wife will have a son." Sarah heard in the tent door, which was behind him. Now Abraham and Sarah were old, well advanced in age. Sarah had passed the age of childbearing. Sarah laughed within herself, saying, "After I have grown old will I have pleasure, my lord being old also?" Yahweh said to Abraham, "Why did Sarah laugh, saying, 'Will I really bear a child when I am old?' Is anything too hard for Yahweh? At the set time I will return to you, when the season comes around, and Sarah will have a son."

COURAGE

Bible quiz: Gideon

1. God allowed the Midianites to attack the Israelites because the Israelites had done evil in the eyes of God. They had turned away from Him and started worshiping other gods (idols)
2. Gideon was threshing wheat in a winepress to hide it from the Midianites
3. The Angel of God called Gideon a "mighty warrior" and told him that the Lord was with him. The Angel informed Gideon that God had chosen him to save Israel from the Midianite
4. Gideon prepared a young goat and unleavened bread as a sacrifice
5. Gideon destroyed the altar of Baal, which his father's family had been worshipping
6. Gideon placed a wool fleece on the ground to receive a sign from God
7. Initially, Gideon had 32,000 soldiers, who were from various tribes of Israel
8. Three hundred men lapped the water with their hands to their mouths
9. Gideon and his army used trumpets, empty jars, and torches to defeat the Midianites
10. The Bible uses the locusts to describe the number of Midianites in their camp

Bible word search puzzle: Gideon's army

Worksheet: What's the Word?

Gideon and the people who were with him rose early and encamped beside the spring of Harod. The camp of Midian was north of them, by the hill of Moreh, in the valley. God said to Gideon, "The people with you are too many for me to give the Midianites into their hand, lest Israel boast over me, saying, 'My own hand has saved me.' Now therefore proclaim in the ears of the people, saying, 'Whoever is fearful and trembling, let him return home and hurry away from Mount Gilead.'" Then 22,000 of the people returned, and 10,000 remained. God said to Gideon, "The people are still too many. Take them down to the water, and I will test them for you there, and anyone of whom I say to you, 'This one shall go with you,' shall go with you, and anyone of whom I say to you, 'This one shall not go with you,' shall not go." So he brought the people down to the water. God said to Gideon, "Every one who laps the water with his tongue, as a dog laps, you shall set by himself. Likewise, every one who kneels down to drink." The number of those who lapped, putting their hands to their mouths, was 300 men, but the rest of the people knelt down to drink water. God said to Gideon, "With the 300 men who lapped I will save you and give the Midianites into your hand, and let all the others go every man to his home." So the people took provisions in their hands, and their trumpets. And he sent the rest of Israel every man to his tent, but retained the 300 men.

TRUST

Bible quiz: Ruth & Naomi

1. Elimelech and his family moved to Moab because of a severe famine in Bethlehem
2. Elimelech died in Moab, leaving Naomi and their two sons
3. Naomi's sons married Moabite women named Orpah and Ruth
4. Naomi decided to return to Bethlehem when she heard that God had ended the famine there
5. Both Orpah and Ruth initially refused to leave Naomi and wanted to go with her to Bethlehem
6. Naomi told them to return because she had no more sons to become their husbands
7. Ruth said, "Where you go I will go, and where you lodge I will lodge. Your people shall be my people, and your God my God."
8. Orpah stayed in Moab, while Ruth decided to accompany Naomi to Bethlehem
9. The people of Bethlehem were surprised and stirred when Naomi and Ruth returned
10. Ruth showed her loyalty and trust to Naomi by insisting on staying with her, despite Naomi's insistence that she return to her people in Moab

Bible word search puzzle: Ruth & Naomi

Worksheet: What's the Word?

Naomi said to her two daughters-in-law, "Go, return each of you to her mother's house. May God deal kindly with you, as you have dealt with the dead and with me. God grant that you may find rest, each of you in the house of her husband!" She kissed them, and they lifted up their voices and wept. They said to her, "No, we will return with you to your people." But Naomi said, "Turn back, my daughters; why will you go with me? Have I yet sons in my womb that they may become your husbands? Turn back, my daughters; go your way, for I am too old to have a husband. If I should say I have hope, even if I should have a husband this night and should bear sons, would you therefore wait till they were grown? Would you therefore refrain from marrying? No, my daughters, for it is exceedingly bitter to me for your sake that the hand of God has gone out against me." They lifted up their voices and wept again. Orpah kissed her mother-in-law, but Ruth clung to her. And she said, "See, your sister-in-law has gone back to her people and to her gods; return after your sister-in-law." But Ruth said, "Do not urge me to leave you or to return from following you. For where you go I will go, and where you lodge I will lodge. Your people shall be my people, and your God my God. Where you die I will die, and there will I be buried. May God do so to me and more also if anything but death parts me from you."

PERSEVERANCE

Bible quiz: Nehemiah

1. Kingdom of Persia
2. Cup-bearer to the king of Persia
3. From Hanani and certain men of Judah
4. Nehemiah asked the king of Persia for permission to return to Jerusalem and rebuild the city walls
5. They accused Nehemiah of turning against the king

6. Eliashib was the high priest
7. The priests
8. It took the Israelites 52 days to rebuild the walls
9. The Israelites' enemies lost their courage because they knew God had helped the Israelites rebuild the walls
10. Feast of Sukkot (Tabernacles)

Bible word search puzzle: Rebuilding of Jerusalem

Worksheet: What's the Word?

When our enemies heard that it was known to us and that God had frustrated their plan, we all returned to the wall, each to his work. From that day on, half of my servants worked on construction, and half held the spears, shields, bows, and coats of mail. And the leaders stood behind the whole house of Judah, who were building on the wall. Those who carried burdens were loaded in such a way that each labored on the work with one hand and held his weapon with the other. And each of the builders had his sword strapped at his side while he built. The man who sounded the trumpet was beside me. I said to the nobles and to the officials and to the rest of the people, "The work is great and widely spread, and we are separated on the wall, far from one another. In the place where you hear the sound of the trumpet, rally to us there. Our God will fight for us." So, we labored at the work, and half of them held the spears from the break of dawn until the stars came out. I also said to the people at that time, "Let every man and his servant pass the night within Jerusalem, that they may be a guard for us by night and may labor by day." So, neither I nor my brothers nor my servants nor the men of the guard who followed me, none of us took off our clothes…

INTEGRITY
Bible quiz: The story of Job
1. Job and his family lived in the land of Uz
2. Before his trials, Job had ten children (seven sons, three daughters)

3. A house fell on Job's children
4. "Have you considered My servant, Job; there is none like him on the earth."
5. Job's wife encouraged him to curse God
6. Job's friends sat in silence for seven days and seven nights
7. Job's friends gave him money and a ring of gold
8. God answered Job out of a whirlwind
9. Leviathan lived in the sea
10. God gave Job twice as much as he had before

Bible word search puzzle: The righteous man's trials

Worksheet: What's the Word?

There was a day when the sons of God came to present themselves before Him, and Satan also came among them to present himself before God. And God said to Satan, "From where have you come?" Satan answered God and said, "From going to and fro on the earth, and from walking up and down on it." God said to Satan, "Have you considered my servant Job, that there is none like him on the earth, a blameless and upright man, who fears God and turns away from evil? He still holds fast his integrity, although you incited me against him to destroy him without reason." Satan answered God and said, "Skin for skin! All that a man has he will give for his life. But stretch out your hand and touch his bone and his flesh, and he will curse you to your face." God said to Satan, "Behold, he is in your hand; only spare his life." So, Satan went out from the presence of God and struck Job with loathsome sores from the sole of his foot to the crown of his head. And he took a piece of broken pottery with which to scrape himself while he sat in the ashes. Then his wife said to him, "Do you still hold fast your integrity? Curse God and die." But he said to her, "You speak as one of the foolish women would speak. Shall we receive good from God, and shall we not receive evil?" In all this Job did not sin with his lips.

COMPASSION
Bible quiz: Feeding the 5000
1. The young boy had two fish and five barley loaves
2. 5000 men, plus women and children
3. Lake Tiberius
4. On a hill (mountain) near the Sea of Galilee
5. To test Philip
6. Yeshua blessed the bread
7. Twelve baskets were filled with leftovers
8. This event took place in Galilee
9. The Feast of Unleavened Bread
10. Yeshua went away to a mountain by Himself to pray

Bible word search puzzle: Feeding the 5000

Worksheet: What's the Word?
Now when Yeshua heard this, He withdrew from there in a boat to a desolate place by Himself. But when the crowds heard it, they followed Him on foot from the towns. When He went ashore He saw a great crowd, and He had compassion on them and healed their sick. Now when it was evening, the disciples came to Him and said, "This is a desolate place, and the day is now over; send the crowds away to go into the villages and buy food for themselves." But Yeshua said, "They need not go away; you give them something to eat." They said to Him, "We have only five loaves here and two fish." And He said, "Bring them here to Me." Then He ordered the crowds to sit down on the grass, and taking the five loaves and the two fish, He looked up to heaven and said a blessing. Then He broke the loaves and gave them to the disciples, and the disciples gave them to the crowds. And they all ate and were satisfied. And they took up twelve baskets full of the broken pieces left over. And those who ate were about five thousand men, besides women and children.

RESPONSIBILITY
Bible quiz: Noah builds an ark
1. The Nephilim (giants)
2. Righteous
3. God regretted making man on earth because man's wickedness was great
4. Noah's sons were Shem, Ham, and Japheth
5. God told Noah to build an ark
6. 300 cubits long, 50 cubits wide, and 30 cubits high
7. The ark had one window
8. The ark had three decks
9. God planned to destroy everything on earth with a flood
10. God said that He would establish His covenant with Noah

Bible word search puzzle: Noah's ark

Worksheet: What's the Word?
Make yourself an ark of gopher wood. Make rooms in the ark, and cover it inside and out with pitch. This is how you are to make it: the length of the ark 300 cubits, its breadth 50 cubits, and its height 30 cubits. Make a roof for the ark, and finish it to a cubit above, and set the door of the ark in its side. Make it with lower, second, and third decks. For behold, I will bring a flood of waters upon the earth to destroy all flesh in which is the breath of life under heaven. Everything that is on the earth shall die. But I will establish my covenant with you, and you shall come into the ark, you, your sons, your wife, and your sons' wives with you. And of every living thing of all flesh, you shall bring two of every sort into the ark to keep them alive with you. They shall be male and female. Of the birds according to their kinds, and of the animals according to their kinds, of every creeping thing of the ground, according to its kind, two of every sort shall come in to you to keep them alive. Also take with you every sort of food that is eaten, and store it up. It shall serve as food for you and for them." Noah did this; he did all that God commanded him.

SELF-CONTROL
Bible quiz: David spares Saul's life
1. Saul had returned from following the Philistines
2. Saul chose three thousand men out of all Israel to help him find David
3. Saul went into the cave to relieve himself
4. David and his men were sitting in the innermost parts of the cave
5. David cut off a corner of Saul's robe
6. David forbid his men to attack Saul
7. David bowed his face to the earth and paid Saul respect
8. Saul wept
9. The Kingdom of Israel
10. After they met, Saul went home and David went up to the stronghold

Bible word search puzzle: David spares Saul's life

Worksheet: What's the Word?
When Saul returned from following the Philistines, he was told, "Behold, David is in the wilderness of Engedi." Saul took three thousand chosen men out of all Israel and went to find David and his men in front of the Wildgoats' Rocks. He came to the sheepfolds where there was a cave, and went in to relieve himself. Now David and his men were sitting in the innermost parts of the cave. And David's men said to him, "Here is the day of which God said to you, 'Behold, I will give your enemy into your hand, and you shall do to him as it shall seem good to you.'" Then David arose and stealthily cut off a corner of Saul's robe. But afterwards, David's heart struck him because he had cut off a corner of Saul's robe. He said to his men, "God forbid that I should do this thing to my lord, who is God's anointed, to put my hand against him, seeing he is God's anointed." David persuaded his men with these words and did not permit them to attack Saul. And Saul left the cave and went on his way.

DILIGENCE
Bible quiz: Elijah & Elisha
1. Gilgal
2. Bethel
3. Elisha refused, vowing not to leave Elijah
4. The sons of the prophets at Bethel and Jericho warned Elisha
5. Elijah used his cloak to part the waters of the Jordan River
6. Elisha asked for a double portion of Elijah's spirit
7. Elijah was taken up to Heaven in a whirlwind, with chariots of fire and horses of fire separating him and Elisha
8. Elisha tore his own clothes in two pieces in grief
9. Elisha struck the water with the cloak, causing it to part so he could cross on dry ground
10. The sons of the prophets came to meet Elisha and bowed to the ground before him

Bible word search puzzle: Elijah taken to Heaven

Worksheet: What's the Word?
Elijah said to Elisha, "Stay here, for God has sent me as far as Bethel." Elisha said, "As God lives, and as you live, I will not leave you." So they went down to Bethel. The sons of the prophets who were in Bethel came out to Elisha and said to him, "Do you know that today God will take away your master from over you?" And he said, "Yes, I know it; keep quiet." Elijah said to him, "Elisha, please stay here, for God has sent me to Jericho." But he said, "As God lives, and as you yourself live, I will not leave you." So they came to Jericho. The sons of the prophets who were at Jericho drew near to Elisha and said to him, "Do you know that today God will take away your master from over you?" And he answered, "Yes, I know it; keep quiet." Then Elijah said to him, "Stay here, for God has sent me to the Jordan." But he said, "As God lives, and as you yourself live, I will not leave you." So the two of them went on. Fifty men of the sons of the prophets

also went and stood at some distance from them, as they both were standing by the Jordan. Elijah took his cloak, rolled it up and struck the water. The water was parted to the one side and to the other, till the two of them could go over on dry ground. When they had crossed, Elijah said to Elisha, "Ask what I shall do for you, before I am taken away." Elisha said, "Let there be a double portion of your spirit on me." And he said, "You have asked a hard thing; yet, if you see me as I am being taken from you, it shall be so for you. But if you do not see me, it shall not be so." As they still went on and talked, behold, chariots and horses of fire separated the two of them. And Elijah went up by a whirlwind into heaven.

RESILIENCE
Bible quiz: Paul and Barnabas visit Lystra
1. The man had been crippled since he was born
2. Paul said to the crippled man, "Stand upright on your feet."
3. The crippled man stood up and began to walk
4. Paul was called Hermes
5. Barnabas was called Zeus
6. At the entrance to the city
7. Paul and Barnabas tore their clothes and tried to teach the crowd about God
8. Jews from Antioch and Iconium persuaded the crowds to stone Paul
9. Paul stood up and walked back into the city of Lystra
10. Paul and Barnabas traveled to Derbe

Bible crossword puzzle: False gods!

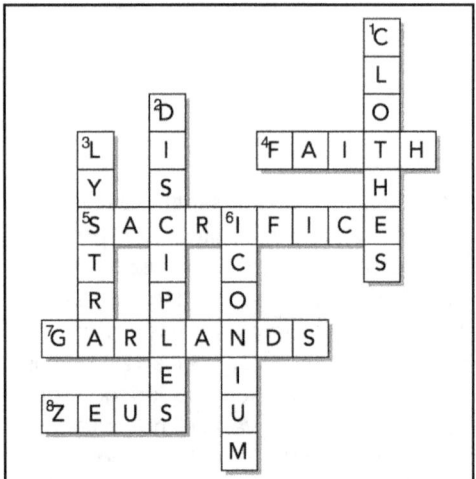

Worksheet: What's the Word?
When the crowds saw what Paul had done, they lifted up their voices, saying in Lycaonian, "The gods have come down to us in the likeness of men!" Barnabas they called Zeus, and Paul, Hermes, because he was the chief speaker. And the priest of Zeus, whose temple was at the entrance to the city, brought oxen and garlands to the gates and wanted to offer sacrifice with the crowds. But when the apostles Barnabas and Paul heard of it, they tore their garments and rushed out into the crowd, crying out, "Men, why are you doing these things? We also are men, of like nature with you, and we bring you good news, that you should turn from these vain things to a living God, who made the heaven and the earth and the sea and all that is in them. In past generations he allowed all the nations to walk in their own ways. Yet he did not leave himself without witness, for he did good by giving you rains from heaven and fruitful seasons, satisfying your hearts with food and gladness." Even with these words they scarcely restrained the people from offering sacrifice to them. But Jews came from Antioch and Iconium, and having persuaded the crowds, they stoned Paul and dragged him out of the city, supposing that he was dead. But when the disciples gathered about him, he rose up and entered the city, and on the next day he went on with Barnabas to Derbe.

◆◇ DISCOVER MORE ACTIVITY BOOKS! ◇◆

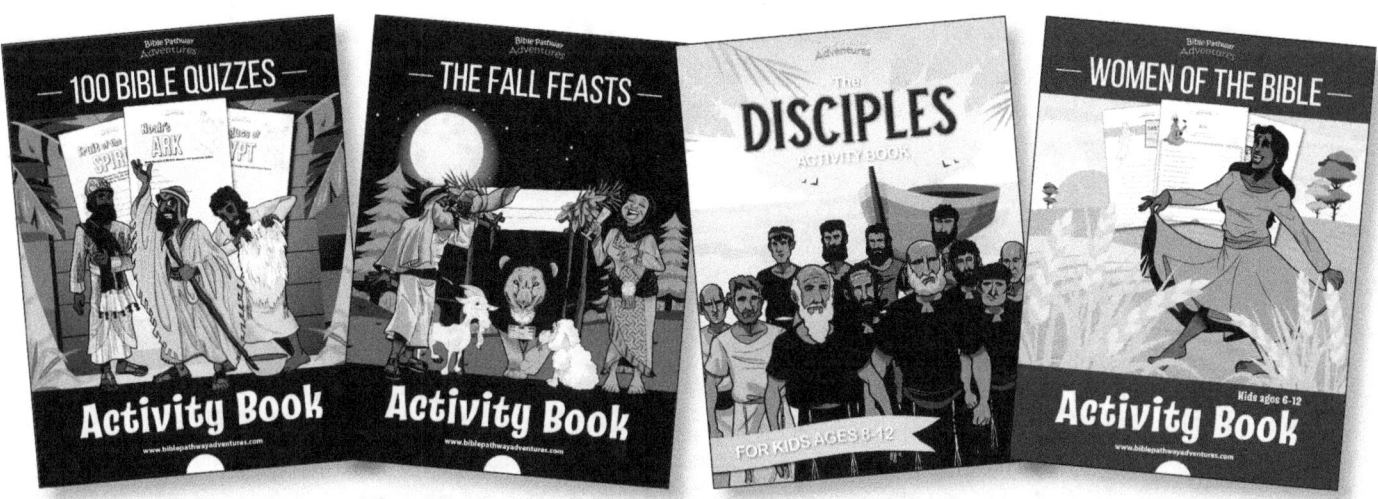

Available for purchase at shop.biblepathwayadventures.com

INSTANT DOWNLOAD!

100 Bible Quizzes
The Fall Feasts
The Disciples
Women of the Bible

Paul's Journeys
Moses Ten Plagues
Fruit of the Spirit
Miracles of the Bible